GIBBER FAMILY EDITION

Torah Beloved
Reflections on the Love of Torah and
the Celebration of the Holiday of Matan Torah

GIBBER FAMILY EDITION

Torah Beloved

Reflections on the Love of
Torah and the Celebration of
the Holiday of Matan Torah

by
Norman Lamm

EDITED BY
Daniel Gober

KTAV PUBLISHING HOUSE

TORAH BELOVED:
Reflections on the Love of Torah and
the Celebration of the Holiday of Matan Torah

OU PRESS
an imprint of the Orthodox Union
11 Broadway
New York, NY 10004
www.oupress.org

KTAV PUBLISHING HOUSE
527 Empire Blvd
Brooklyn, NY 11225
www.ktav.com
orders@ktav.com
Ph: (718) 972-5449 / Fax: (718) 972-6307

Copyright © 2020 Norman Lamm

"Scholarship and Piety" used with permission of KTAV
Publishing House and Rabbi Norman Lamm.

"Knowing vs. Learning: Which Takes Precedence?" used with
permission of ATID (Academy for Torah Initiatives and Directions).

All rights reserved. No part of this publication may be reproduced,
stored in a retrieval system or transmitted in any form or by
any means, electronic, mechanical, photocopying or otherwise,
without the prior permission of the publisher except in the case
of brief quotations embedded in critical articles or reviews.

Typeset in Arno Pro by Raphaël Freeman, Renana Typesetting

ISBN 978-1-60280-387-9

Printed and bound in the United States of America

Dedicated in Honor of

Rabbi Dr. Norman and Mindy Lamm

Mentors, role models, and sources of inspiration
for our family and the entire Jewish community

Elliot and Debbie Gibber and Family

Dedicated in Loving Memory of
Gloria Mehler *z"l*

Lover of the Word and the word.
A pious woman, steeped in
Torah study, prayer, and kindness.
At home in shul, the library, and the study hall.
Enthusiastic scholar, voracious reader,
and loyal and loving daughter, niece,
sister, aunt, and friend.

By her family

Norman and Mindy Lamm
Howie and Razy Baruch
Akiva and Bracha Berger
Steve and Esther Blumenfrucht
Ari Goldman and Shira Dicker
Bobby Dratch
Mark and Rachel Dratch
Sam and Sari Dratch
Yaakov and Yolly Faratci
Yigal and Tamar Gross
Ted and Tova Halperin
Stu and Ahuva Halpern
Dan and Ariela Harcsztark
Eitan and Peninah Kaplansky
Avraham and Liora Kelman
Herbert Kelman

Shalom and Syma Kelman
Jonathan and Debra Kolitz
Ari and Shlomit Lamm
Daniel Lamm
Devorah Lamm
Josh and Rivkie Lamm
Shalom and Tina Lamm
Shmuel and Sara Lamm
Yehuda and Angela Lamm
Yoni Lamm
Yinon and Penina Levy
Dovid Mehler
Shalom and Elaine Mehler
Tzvi and Tova Sinensky
David and Chaye Warburg
Gordon Mehler and Ariel Zwang

Contents

Editor's Preface	xi
Introduction	xv
Foreword	xix

LOVE OF TORAH

1: What Is Torah?	3
2: How to Read the Torah	9
3: The Senses of Torah	19
4: Strange Medicine	25
5: The Arrogance of Modernism	33
6: A Premature Obituary and an Immature Religion	39
7: Why Moral People Need Torah	43
8: The Other Revelation	51
9: The Age of Gemini	59
10: Judaism as an Alternative	67
11: Orthodoxy and Fundmentalism	75
12: A Step Backwards in the Right Direction	85
13: In the Days of Smallness	91

CELEBRATING SHAVUOT

14: This Very Day	99
15: Shavuot Derives from Shevua	109
16: Waiting	117
17: How Do You Know You're Awake?	125
18: On the Look-Out	131
19: The Little Things	137
20: To Be a Ruth-Like Jew	143
21: Who Is the Missing Relative?	151
22: Four Steps	159

APPENDIX

Scholarship and Piety	167
Knowing vs. Learning: Which Takes Precedence?	207

Editor's Preface

IT IS A GREAT PRIVILEGE FOR ME TO EDIT THIS VOLUME of sermons and essays of Rabbi Norman Lamm. I must admit that I have never met Rabbi Lamm in person and have not had the privilege of experiencing his well-known powerful delivery – I can only imagine how incredible an experience that was for his congregants. After reading previous books of Rabbi Lamm's sermons such as *The Royal Table*, and the *Derashot Ledorot* series, I was caught in his web – and found myself returning to the Yeshiva University Lamm Heritage website to read more of his sermons.

Every week, I read his sermons for each *parasha* and I was amazed at his ability to use the words of the Tanakh and Ḥazal to gain insight into human nature and explain the fundamentals of Torah with such precision and clarity. I quickly found myself sharing his thoughts and insights with my close friends every week. Sure enough, they also shared my interest and excitement at this master *darshan*'s words. It was clear that these words, though written a *yovel* ago, resonate so effectively to the modern ear.

I was particularly attracted to a theme that Rabbi Lamm came back to so often throughout his sermons – the love of Torah. I found that Rabbi Lamm's sermons that relate to the love of Torah were not yet included in previous volumes of his sermons, and I have collected them here. Very little editing was necessary, further testimony to the precision and clarity of the original delivery. The titles of the individual meditations are those originally used by Rabbi Lamm, but the title to the volume as a whole is our proposal. The sermons were lightly edited, some missing sources added, and a few current events side comments in the original sermons were not included here. All but one of the sermons are presented in the same textual format as the original PDF except for *A Premature Obituary and Immature Religion*, which has been adapted from bullet-point format for essay presentation. In addition to Rabbi Lamm's sermons, we have included an Appendix containing two previously published essays by Rabbi Lamm in which Rabbi Lamm delves in greater detail into the subject of Torah and appreciation of Torah.

I would like to express *hakarat hatov* to Dr. Joel Wolowelsky for mentoring me through this project. I was fortunate to be a student of Dr. Wolowelsky at Yeshiva of Flatbush twenty years ago and benefit from his mentorship at that time on a personal level. It is truly a privilege for me to collaborate with someone who has contributed so much to the proliferation of Torah publications. As the sermons that appear in this volume were gleaned from the selection on the Lamm Heritage website at Yeshiva University, many thanks go to the former Dean of the Libraries at Yeshiva University, Mrs. Pearl Berger, who initiated the archiving of Rabbi Lamm's documents. I extend gratitude to KTAV Publishing House for their consent to the inclusion of Rabbi Lamm's essay, "Scholarship and Piety," and to ATID (Academy for Torah Initiatives and Directions) for their consent to the inclusion of Rabbi Lamm's essay, "Knowing vs. Learning: Which Takes Precedence?". I would also like to thank OU PRESS and KTAV for publishing *Torah Beloved* and continuing to make Rabbi Lamm's Torah insights available to the next generation of students. And last, I want to express my appreciation to my wife, Jennifer, who works so hard to maintain a home where the love of Torah can flourish. I pray that our four children, Sophie, Jonah, Mia, and Gabriel, can achieve a love of Torah that will enrich their own lives.

It is my sincere hope that *Torah Beloved* will enable every one of us to experience the breadth and depth of Torah as presented by Rabbi Lamm. With the lessons and insights imparted to us by Rabbi Lamm in these sermons and essays, our love of Torah is sure to increase and we will gain a renewed sense of appreciation of Torah. We will then be prepared to successfully meet the challenge of the holiday of Shavuot, which Rabbi Lamm so appropriately describes: "For every Jew must today, as an individual and in a sacred and inviolable personal act, receive the Torah."

Daniel Gober
January 14, 2019

Introduction

IN THIS WONDERFUL BOOK OF SERMONS AND ESSAYS on the subject of our beloved Torah, Rabbi Lamm raises the question of why Shavuot, the holiday celebrating God's bestowal of the gift of Torah to His people, is known as *zeman matan Toratenu*, the time of the giving of the Torah, and not instead as *zeman kabbalat Toratenu*, the time in which we received the Torah. With his customary rhetorical skill, Rabbi Lamm offers and elaborates upon an insight of one of the Hasidic masters, who explained that while the Torah was given only once by God, its reception differs for each and every Jew. Shavuot celebrates the gift, but it is up to each one of us to embrace it and receive it based on our unique capabilities.

I would like to suggest another approach to answer this question. The reason we do not refer to Shavuot as the day on which we received the Torah is that Shavuot is *not* the day on which we received the Torah. Before I am accused of heresy, let me clarify. The *Luḥot* which Moshe received on Shavuot were shattered at the base of the mountain, forty days later. We never received them. It was only after two more forty-day periods of prayer and fasting, on Yom Kippur, that God gave Moshe the second set of *Luḥot* which the Jewish people were able to receive, unshattered. Thus, the day on which we received the Torah is actually Yom Kippur, not Shavuot, and that is why Shavuot is not identified in our liturgy as the day we received the Torah.

This, however, raises another question. If Shavuot is not the day on which we received the Torah, what is it that we are celebrating on Shavuot? The answer to this question is based on another well-known question. In the *Dayenu* song in the Haggadah, we recite: *Ilu karavnu lifnei Har Sinai velo natan lanu et haTorah, dayenu, Had He brought us close before Har Sinai, but not given us the Torah, it would have been enough for us*. What exactly would we have to be thankful for had we been brought to Har Sinai but not given the Torah?

Of course, the answer is that we are thankful for the very experience of Sinai, the encounter with God which imprinted itself upon every Jewish soul for all eternity. This too is what we celebrate on Shavuot, the day on which the Torah was given, with the accompanying *kolot uvrakim ve'anan kaved al hahar*, "thunder, lightning, and dense cloud upon the mountain" (*Shemot* 19:16). In other words, on Shavuot we celebrate the day on which the entire Jewish people experienced God, on which we obtained the metaphysical and spiritual experience of Torah, if not the Torah itself.

The Gemara (*Horayot* 12a) tells us that kings are anointed alongside a spring of water, so that their reigns will continue like the constantly flowing spring. The Gemara continues with Rav Mesharshiya's instructions to his son to study alongside the water so that his studies will continue like the constantly flowing spring. The connection between anointing a king and studying Torah is difficult to understand; however, if we keep in mind Maimonides' "three crowns," the connection becomes apparent (*Hilkhot Talmud Torah* 3:1):

> Three crowns were conferred upon Israel: the crown of Torah, the crown of priesthood, and the crown of royalty. Aaron merited the crown of priesthood... David merited the crown of royalty... The crown of Torah is set aside, waiting, and ready for each Jew... Whoever desires may come and take it. Lest you say that the other crowns surpass the crown of Torah, the verse (Proverbs 8:15–16) states:

"By me, kings reign, princes decree justice, and nobles rule." Thus, you have learned that the crown of Torah is greater than the other two.

Torah scholarship too is a crown, which surpasses the crown of kingship. Students of Torah are endowed with a unique majesty, greater than that of earthly kings, and they too should therefore take steps to ensure the continuity of their heritage. Throughout his distinguished rabbinic career as well as in his leadership of Yeshiva University, Rabbi Lamm has communicated this theme of the majestic quality of Torah study. This volume as well expresses the grandeur and the majesty of the Torah and of *Talmud Torah*, and the encounter with the Divine which is contained within this experience. With his eloquence and understanding, Rabbi Lamm conveys what learning Torah and loving Torah means.

Many dedicated individuals were involved in the preparation of this volume. My esteemed friend, Dr. Joel B. Wolowelsky, provided the guidance and impetus to bring this project to successful fruition. Daniel Gober, the editor of this volume, selected the sermons and ably prepared them for publication. I would like to acknowledge as well my colleagues at OU PRESS. Mrs. Yocheved Goldberg carefully reviewed and copyedited the manuscript; Rabbi Eliyahu Krakowski provided editorial assistance; and Rabbi Simon Posner supervised all aspects of the editing and production of this edition. This project could not have been realized without the generous support of our sponsors. We are most grateful to the Gibber family for their generous support and their ongoing commitment to Rabbi Lamm, as well as to the family of Gloria Mehler, *z"l*, for their assistance. All those who participated in this project can be justifiably proud of their contribution to *Klal Yisrael* which this volume represents.

Menachem Dov Genack
General Editor
OU PRESS

Foreword

SEVERAL YEARS AGO, I WAS SIFTING THROUGH A CACHE of old correspondence kept by my grandfather and teacher, Rabbi Norman Lamm. Perusing through folders of miscellany, I suddenly came across a letter he had written to a young girl named Laurie, then a member of his congregation at The Jewish Center in Manhattan.

Laurie was a lovely child. She delighted in the synagogue atmosphere, and so was regularly in attendance. More than anything, however, she adored a sweet little pet bird that she kept at home.

One Shabbat, my grandfather noticed that Laurie was absent from the services. He observed a similar pattern over the next few weeks. Concerned, he placed a call to her home only to discover that Laurie's bird has passed away. Distraught over the loss of her companion, my grandfather learned, Laurie could not summon the energy to return to synagogue.

Even as he presided over a *shul* patronized by hundreds – and maintained responsibilities as a public intellectual and first-rate theologian besides – my grandfather dropped everything. Shutting himself in his office, he labored long and hard over a three-page, personal letter to Laurie eulogizing her beloved pet. I present to you the letter's remarkable conclusion:

> This sad occasion should give you pause for thought – as it does for me while I am writing this letter – about how very much we have to do in the time that God has allotted

us. We have so much to achieve, so much love to show, so many mitzvot to perform, so much happiness and pride to give our parents and grandparents!

When you look at it that way, you will see that the fact that life ends is not all bad, even if it certainly isn't all good. That is why we Jews recite a special blessing at the occasion of death or any kind of very bad news. We say *barukh Dayan ha'emet* – "blessed is the true Judge." God is a judge in the sense that He sometimes pronounces a harsh verdict and sentences one of His beloved creatures to death. But He is also "true" – and what He does, He does out of love and kindness as well. He knows that by taking away life, He gives us the opportunity to fill the time we do have with all the good things that make life worth living.

I know, Laurie, that losing the bird was a painful experience, but I hope that the explanation I gave you will help you in some way to accept the fact with less anguish. If the death of that little bird will help you achieve this kind of perspective, then that little bird will itself have made a real contribution to your life – and in that way, it will live on!

It is this simple, delicate pathos that defines my grandfather. He has always understood, better than anyone I have ever known, that the bedrock upon which great Jewish leadership rests is neither political stature nor analytical legerdemain, but rather a deep and abiding concern for the wellbeing and spiritual health of every single person under one's care.

His compassionate breadth of spirit expresses itself as well in the sort of Torah he taught during the many decades he spent at the helm of the Jewish community. Among proponents and practitioners of *derush* – homiletics – over the last hundred years, he is quite nearly unrivaled. In his manifesto promoting the virtues of *derush*, "Notes of an Unrepentant Darshan," he proclaimed, "If *halakhah* is the science of Jewish religious life, *derush* is its art, and esthetics needs no apology in its claim to a rightful place in the sanctuary of Torah."

It is no coincidence that *derush* – Torah's art; its poetry – spoke so profoundly to my grandfather. For it is poetry's special task to capture the ineffable truths of the human experience and implant them in our hearts and souls. It is not through science, but only through the arts that we may put a name to things like love, fear, faith, doubt, cruelty and kindness – in short, the things that make us human. *Derush* speaks to that essential humanity in each of us, and so compels the *darshan* to focus upon the needs of his listeners. What is on their minds? What are their hopes and their dreams? Unlike the *posek* who assumes the magisterial role of the authority dispensing justice, the *darshan* strikes the far more modest, but equally essential pose of the servant slaking the spiritual thirst of his listeners. Some listeners will need a learned disquisition on the perils of assimilation, or a dissertation on the state of American Orthodoxy. But others, like Laurie, will need simple words of comfort upon the loss of a cherished childhood companion.

The greatness of Rabbi Norman Lamm lies in his ability and willingness to provide all of these with equal grace and sagacity. To paraphrase King Solomon's sublime words (Proverbs 31:26), "He opens his mouth with wisdom, and on his tongue is the teaching of kindness."

May the merit of this wonderful volume of characteristically brilliant and compassionate *derush* vouchsafe my grandfather many happy and healthy years ahead.

Ari Lamm
13 Nisan 5779

"O How I love Your Torah!
All day long it is my conversation."

☙

(PSALMS 119:97)

Love of Torah

One
What Is Torah?*

A GREAT HASIDIC RABBI ONCE EXPLAINED WHY SHAVUOT is known as *zeman matan Toratenu*, the time of the *giving* of the Torah, and not as *zeman kabbalat Toratenu*, the time of the *receiving* of the Torah. He said that the reason was that God gave the Torah to all Jews equally. There was one *matan*, one giving. But it is up to each Jew to receive the Torah, and each one receives a different amount and on a different level of understanding. There are thus as many "receivings" of Torah as there are Jews. Hence, Shavuot is the *zeman matan* and not *zeman kabbalat haTorah*. For every Jew must today, as an individual and in a sacred and inviolable personal act, receive the Torah.

So we are now prepared, each one of us, to receive the gift of God, the Torah. We must therefore know what Torah is. What, in short, does Torah mean? What does it mean to us? What does it mean to each and every individual here? Allow me to give a number of impressions as to what Torah is, so that perhaps one person here will see it in a new light, and receive the Torah anew.

Torah is an inheritance. "The Torah Moses commanded us is the heritage of the congregation of Jacob" (Deuteronomy 33:4).

---

* June 7, 1954

It is a legacy left to us by parents, grandparents and forebears since the beginning of time. In it are recorded the annals of man's greatness as well as his depravity. Towering saints like Moses move through its sacred script even as petty scoundrels like Balaam worm their way into this all-encompassing picture of man on earth. It is the chain of tradition which links us with all the giants of history whose blood pulsates through our own veins at this very moment. It links us to primitive Adam as he was formed out of the bowels of the Earth. It unites us with Abraham as he stands before God debating with the Almighty for the rescue of evil Sodom. It puts aside the patriarch Jacob as he wrangles with his angelic opponent before the break of dawn upon the distant plains of Mesopotamia. It makes us feel part of the Israelites who cross the Red Sea and then enter Canaan. In short, as our inheritance of ages gone by, it spans the abyss of Time unto the dim Past, makes us sure of the distant Future, and unites all Time in the moment we receive it, the Torah of the Eternal.

Torah is truth. "Blessed are You... who has given us the Torah of truth..." (blessing after reading the Torah). It is not a high-sounding document written to impress others. It is the declaration of divine truth. It is the antithesis of the propagandist and the nemesis of the demagogue. For it teaches that truth must reign above all, and that none – not even the greatest, not even a Moses – is free from the searching, critical beam of Truth. It is the comfort of those who fear the searing comments of the cynics. For it teaches that Truth can be attained in this world. Hasidim commented that God began the creation of the world with truth. And they proved it by taking the last 3 letters of the first 3 words of the Bible, the words describing the first creation, *"Bereshit bara Elokim* – In the beginning God created" (Genesis 1:1). The letters are *alef, mem, taf – emet,* or truth, so that Truth is the beginning and end of the world. And it therefore can be attained.

Torah is peace. "Its ways are ways of pleasantness, and all its paths are peace" (Proverbs 3:17). It teaches that peace, *shalom*, is so important that the very word becomes a name of God. It gives us the Sabbath – the embodiment of true peace the world over, and the insurance of *shalom bayit*, domestic peace. For what is the lighting of the Sabbath candles if not an invitation to husband and wife to live in peace and harmony? It outlaws murder. It prohibits wanton destruction. It forbids *sinat ḥinam*, hatred. It commands neighborly love. A Torah of this sort, if followed, can prevent hot wars and cold wars, atom wars and hydrogen wars, germ wars and any kind of war. It has raised, in its sphere of influence, a people known as Jews, whose first greeting and whose parting message, at all times and places, is one and the same – *shalom*, peace. It is therefore the only hope of a world tottering on the brink of disaster and frantically rushing towards mass suicide in better and bigger wars.

Torah is the equality of all men before God. "One law shall there be for the native and the proselyte who lives among you" (Exodus 12:49). There is no oligarchy or aristocracy in the Torah. The rich man is not a privileged character. He is equal with his impoverished fellow man before the God who created both from the same lowly origin, and endowed both with the same lofty soul. The Torah does not discriminate in favor of the poorer class or the labor and proletariat class. Equality is a two-way equation. "Nor shall you show deference to a poor man in his dispute" (Exodus 23:3). It teaches that man was created one, so that none of his descendants may lay claim to greater *yiḥus*, lineage, than any others. It frowns upon slavery, for the man who voluntarily enters into servitude demeans the divine image in which he was created, and makes himself inferior to one whom God deemed his equal. And yet the Torah still maintains his equality with his master. So that if a master has only one pillow in the house, it is the slave who sleeps on it, for the slave must be treated no worse than the master.

Torah is knowledge. "... and in His Torah he meditates day and night" (Psalms 1:2). It is the greatest work of law of all time. Its ethical and moral precepts are embodied not only in its sweeping universal aspects, but in every small detail of which it speaks. It contains all knowledge in it, one way or another. "Search it and search it, for all is contained in it" (Avot – Ethics of Our Fathers 5:25). The Torah described creation on an evolutionary pattern thirty centuries before Darwin. It described hygienic precautions before Pasteur's France was inhabited by human beings. It warned against and described the sort of destruction that can be achieved only with hydrogen bombs before man even began to suspect that such great forces existed in nature. Its laws have occupied legions of scholars, from the Sanhedrin of King David, through the House of Hillel, through the academies of Babylon, to the *yeshivot* of Poland and Lithuania, and the contemporary Talmudic schools of America and Israel. And through all this, its greatest knowledge that it has to offer is the greatest knowledge Man can aspire to. And that is: the knowledge of God. For how did the Gerrer Rebbe put it? In his comments on the verse (Deuteronomy 4:39), "And you shall *know* this day, and enshrine it in your heart, that the Lord is God of Heaven and Earth, there is no other" – meaning, there is no other god. But the Gerrer Rebbe says: And you shall know that the Lord is God, *there is no other knowledge*. No, there is no other knowledge. For without this there is nothing for Man to know. And when he knows this, he knows all there is worth knowing.

Torah is unfathomable perfection. "The Torah of *Hashem* is perfect, restoring the soul..." (Psalms 19:8). How can man hope to fully comprehend that which was written by God Almighty? For the Torah is perfect, and man is of necessity imperfect. It is so holy, so lofty, so beyond us, that man can never hope to fully grasp it. It was the immortal Baal Shem Tov who said: we so often think that we have delved into the core and heart of

Torah. And yet, it is perfect, that is, even its surface hasn't been scratched yet...

Torah is life itself. "It is a tree of life to those who grasp it" (Proverbs 3:18). Without it, life is one meaningless drudgery, an endless and eternal wandering in a circle, never reaching any real goal for there has never been one. With it, life takes on new meaning, gains purpose and is elevated to holiness. Without it, life is only a flash in the pan, a passing shadow, a cloud blown by, a leaf driven deep into nowhere. For it is soon over and done with. With it, there is immortality, eternal life, for the Torah is the cement which binds man with God and thus awards him endlessness. But there is always this condition attached to the life-giving quality of Torah: "to those who grasp it" (Proverbs 3:18, recited upon returning the Torah to the ark). We must hold tight, take it into our homes, our hearts, and clutch it to our souls. When the Torah is received, man is reborn, he gets a brand-new life. For did not our Rabbis tell us that at the foot of Mount Sinai, when God gave Israel its greatest treasure, the Torah, the angels stopped their singing, the winds stopped blowing, the seas froze in their places, animals ceased their noises, the heavens stopped in its path, and the souls of all Israel left them? Aye, their souls left them, their old souls passed away, and instead they received new, more precious souls – they were reborn by Torah. We too, then, at this moment that we are *mekabel Torah*, can achieve rebirth, attain meaning in life, assure ourselves of immortality, but only if we grasp and hold hard.

And finally, after mentioning all these lofty things that Torah is, such as truth and peace and inheritance of the ages; equality before God, knowledge, unfathomable perfection and life itself, we might imagine that Torah is something too high, too beholden, too beyond us and above us for us to receive even if we should raise our hands and attempt to grasp.

Yet this just what Torah is not. Our Rabbis say it was not given to angels, but to humans (*Berakhot* 25b). It is precisely this that we must keep in mind if we are to receive the Torah properly. It is our inheritance and our truth; it is the peace of the world and equality for all men; it is our knowledge of God and, though unfathomable perfection, it is a perfection towards which we must strive; it is life, not for angels or divine spirits, but life for you, for me, for our families, for all Israel, for every man, woman and child on the face of earth.

"It is not too hard for you, nor too far from you. It is not in heaven... nor is it beyond the seas... But it is very near unto you, in your mouth and in your heart, that you may do it" (Deuteronomy 30:11–14). For that, friends, is Torah. Near unto you; in thy mouth; in your heart; and, especially, that you may do it.

Two
How to Read the Torah*

THESE COMMENTS ON "HOW TO READ THE TORAH," ARE not meant to be a demonstration of cantillations or a means of training formal Torah readers. Rather, they are an attempt to set some guidelines as we begin again the cycle of portions of the Torah. They are intended as well as an introduction to our various adult classes, as all Jews begin their annual renewal of the study of Torah.

At one point in today's *parasha*, we read "This is the book of the generations of man" (Genesis 5:1). Most commentators take that to mean not "book" in the formal sense of a volume, but as a listing of the generations that derived from Adam. Nachmanides, however, takes the word "book" literally and tells us that it refers to the entire Torah, which is the "book of the generations of man." Torah is the story of mankind. The Book is apposite to man.

The Kabbala affirms this idea in many ways. For instance, the Zohar (*Zohar Ḥadash Shir HaShirim*, 661 in *Sulam* ed.) maintains that by mystical permutations, the number of souls of Israel present at Sinai is equal to the number of letters in the Torah. Again, we find the equivalence between Book and man.

* October 16, 1971

Hence, the approach to know the Book is akin to that of knowing man. You learn how to understand the "book" from how you understand "man." Books may teach us much about people; but people can tell us more about books. And this is so especially concerning the Book of Books, the Torah.

The first thing that we must learn is respect. In order genuinely to know a man, you must consider him worthy of your study and friendship and concern. If he is not worthy, then your knowledge of him is superficial and unimportant. And what is true of man is true of text, of Torah. At the very least, respect means not to ignore it. To sit in the presence of Torah and not consider it is like staying in the presence of another human being and acting as if he does not exist – and few insults are more humiliating than that. To read Torah, you must be *serious*, and that means – high minded, truly religious. A real student of Torah may never be flippant. You may be puzzled by a *pasuk*, or be put off by a *parasha*, but you must always approach Torah with humility.

The founder of the Chabad movement, R. Shneur Zalman of Liady, in his code of law, gives us an interesting derivation of the custom of Jews to walk with their heads covered (*Shulḥan Arukh Harav, Oraḥ Ḥayyim, siman bet*). The reason is: modesty. Clothing is worn for one of two reasons: warmth or modesty. The head covering is too small to serve for purposes of warmth; it is there for reasons of modesty. It is our way of expressing before God the limitations of our intellectual self-sufficiency. We cover our heads to indicate that we have a degree of bashfulness about our intellectual inadequacy in the face of God. This is how we approach the study of Torah – with respect and humility. This does not mean that what is demanded of us is intellectual capitulation and submission; merely modesty and reverence.

Respect for Torah means also that we must not assume too much about Torah in advance. Do not approach the sacred text with ready-made conclusions. I know people who read a portion of the Torah with a "nothing but" attitude: the Torah is "nothing but" a collection of Middle Eastern myths; "nothing but" a record of early religious superstitions; "nothing but" primitive science; "nothing but" the fear of the unknown expressed magically. With such a presumptuous attitude, you emerge from your encounter with Torah knowing nothing more than the smug prejudices with which you began.

In a sense, I would say that respect means not to get too close to Torah. Despite the fact that Torah is closer to us than anything else – "for it is very near to you" (Deuteronomy 30:14) – you must not get too close to it, you must avoid excessive intimacy, the familiarity which breeds contempt – a fact true both of men and of books. When we are too much "at home" with Torah, when we are "pals" with the text, and we lose the distance which makes both for reverence and perspective, we allow ourselves the liberty of making snap judgments which are unworthy. That is why when we read the Torah we use the silver pointer. Halakha (*Shulḥan Arukh, Oraḥ Ḥayim* 147:1) forbids us to touch the inner part of the Torah scroll. Should we contact the parchment, our hands become unclean (*Shabbat* 14a), and the reason is, primarily, to keep us respectful by forbidding us to handle the sacred scroll directly. We must not lay hands on the Torah; thus we learn to respect it (*Meiri, Megilla* 7b).

The second guideline in how to read the Torah is the awareness of its depth. "This is the book of the generations of man" – just as you do not "read" a man, because he is too complex and deep and requires studying and investigation, analysis and pondering, so it is with Torah. When you say of a man, "I can read him like a book," you diminish his humanity, you reduce him to a manageable automaton subject to manipulation, one whose Pavlovian reactions are all predictable, and hence one who has been depersonalized into a mere mechanism. So if we ask, "How do you read the Torah?" the answer is, "Don't read it! Go much deeper than reading." Reading of the Torah in the synagogue, in its formal sense, with all its carefully prepared melodies and exact text, is only the challenge to what we ought to do, each of us, privately: go deep, ever deeper. It is not enough to read, one must study; it is not enough to *lein* the Torah, one must learn it; it is inadequate to have *keria*, one must have *limud* of the Torah. For both man and Torah are living things, organic beings, and merely reading the Torah is like describing a man's physical qualities; in neither case have I captured the soul, the essence.

That is why our tradition recommends at least four methods of interpretation, the famous *pardes* (*Tikunei Zohar* 71a). It is because we know that there is depth upon depth, layer upon layer, that the various forms of interpretation are valid.

Several years ago, someone wrote a book in which he tried to trace the origins of Freud's seminal idea of depth-psychology, that the human consciousness consists of layer upon layer of awareness, and that we can dig ever deeper until we come to the root of a man's psychic life. This writer (David Bakan) maintained that Freud derived his notions, despite the paucity of his formal Jewish education, from the Jewish ideas which were vaguely, but pervasively, present in his environment. One of these great ideas was that of the Kabbala and its teaching that the Torah must never be understood only on one level, but that it is a mine or reservoir of infinite layers of meaning, and that when you have plumbed one, you must still mine the next, and when you have done the next, you must prepare to dive even deeper to a newer and more profound level of meaning. I do not know if that writer is right or not; I believe he exaggerates. But certainly today we must reverse the direction of the equation. Today we know a great deal about depth-psychology, about the layers of meaning in a man's life. We must now conclude the same about Torah, for this is "the book of the generations of man." What is true of man is true of Torah – depth upon depth, layer upon layer, level beneath level.

The third thing that we must learn in approaching Torah is that with all our scholarly techniques and analysis to probe depth, above all, learning must remain an existential encounter. When you truly know another human being, you know more than the sum of his various parts, his physical description and psychic condition and his clothing and the state of his liver and bile and cardiogram. There is more to man than merely that. There is a sense of mystery. The encounter with him is a genuine experience. Meeting him is what Buber calls an I-Thou relationship. You see him as an equal *gestalt*, not as a mere "it." And so it is with the text of Torah. You must look upon it not as merely an ancient document, not merely as a problem in legal philosophy, not merely as a record of ancient history, but as something living, something dynamic, as an encounter with a "thou," one which preserves and realizes the eternal Thou.

In Hebrew, *daat* means more than just intellectual cognition. "Knowledge" in the biblical scheme means total knowledge, which includes the physical and the spiritual, the material and the psychological and the intellectual. When Adam "knew" his wife Eve (Genesis 4:1), the knowledge covered all areas of human existence, from the sexual to the spiritual. The same word *daat* or knowledge is used for the knowledge of God; it means more than merely a profound grasp of theology or a listing of the philosophical interpretations of the negative attributes of God. It comprehends the totality of existence. So too, we learn from man to book: *daat Torah*, the knowledge of Torah, is more than analysis; it is a profoundly existential meeting with Torah itself. In a word, it is a learning of love.

This encounter of love, both in the case of man and in the case of the book, involves recognition that the one we encounter has absolute individuality, a uniqueness that is irreplaceable. If I know (love) another human being, then I know that person as one who cannot be duplicated, who is utterly different. And the same holds true when I know a passage of Torah.

Furthermore, to know in the sense of love means to want to know more! Maimonides, in the beginning of his great Code, teaches us, concerning the love of God, that when you contemplate the marvels of nature, you begin to love God, and then immediately you are seized with an exceedingly great passion to know the great Name (*Hilkhot Yesodei HaTorah* 2:2). So it is with man too. When you love someone, your desire for knowledge, your appetite for knowing him or her more, is insatiable. The more you know, the more you want to know. And that is precisely the condition that must obtain in Torah. If you study Torah with the right attitude, that of love, you will never be satisfied with what you know; you will always strive for more.

Furthermore, reading or studying Torah with love also sensitizes you to the novelty and surprise that are latent within Torah, to the unpredictably delightful ideas waiting to be conjured up by love and intelligence.

A year or two ago, there appeared a book edited by Eric Marshall and Stuart Hample which was a collection of children's letters to God. One of them, most appropriate to this Sabbath, when we recommence the cycle of the Torah, reads as follows:

> Dear God:
> Maybe you can write some more stories because we've already read everything you have written more than once.
> Thanks in advance.

Some people take that childish attitude with regard to the study of the Torah as we commence Genesis once again: the same stories, the same laws, not a single change. Indeed, should the Torah reader decide to make a single change, we pounce upon him and correct him. The conclusion – it is repetitive and boring. But that is a childish attitude. If our attitude is mature, if we approach Torah with respect, with awareness of its depth, and with love, then the new cycle of *parashot* means for us the anticipation of new discoveries, novel insights, great ideas we have not yet been introduced to.

Fourth, and finally, the right attitude for the study of Torah means that we must read it critically and persistently, using every tool of intelligence and research. To approach Torah with respect and with love does not mean that we can get away with *frumkeit*, with piety alone. A student of Torah must be pious, but piety itself is no guarantee or substitute for scholarship. If you acknowledge that Torah has depth, and you approach Torah with respect and love, you will also want to be deserving of Torah's love and respect in return. As with a human being, if you relate to him or her uncritically, without discrimination and taste, gullibly and simply, you may not find your affections reciprocated. Torah, too, is not satisfied with unsophisticated naiveté. It demands far more from us – a critical attitude, a willingness to meet Torah's problems head on, acumen, and discriminating intelligence.

The Zohar (*Parashat Mishpatim* 95a), in a remarkable passage that sounds as if it were taken out of the courtly tradition of love, compares the Torah to a damsel locked in a castle. The student of Torah, enamored of the princess, marches to and fro, waiting for a glimpse of his beloved. No one recognizes what he is doing there and what goes on in his heart. The damsel occasionally comes to the balcony, shows herself, and quickly returns. He is tempted to look for her and come to the castle. The princess then hides behind the curtain, only letting him occasionally hear her voice. As he pursues his search, she rewards him with an occasional glimpse of her face, challenging her lover to seek her, to discover her. But if the lover (or student of Torah) is discouraged too quickly, if he is impatient, if he ceases his search because he is frustrated, she is annoyed at him and calls out, "Fool!" "A fool believes anything" (Prov. 14:15) – he is uncritical, he can be bluffed!

Torah does not want fools. It does not even want innocent and pious fools. It demands persistence, criticism, determination and intelligence. It wants the brightness that God gave us to be applied to it and its problems, to searching it out, to finding it out.

What real student of Torah does not know of the delight of this flirtatious game played by Torah as part of the romance of the study of the Torah? If you are impatient, if you have no verve, no ambition, then you do not even know that there is a princess in the palace! If you do know it, then by all means, follow the lead, search her out, never stop in your persistent search for Torah and for truth, using every ounce, every fiber of criticism and intelligence. You must follow through the tantalizing leads, the ideas waiting to be exposed, the insights teasingly concealed but anxious to be found out. Torah hides only because she wants you to find her.

These are the four elements in how to read the Torah. Knowledge of the Book is equivalent to the knowledge of man – "This is the book of the generations of man" – in both, genuine knowledge requires respect; awareness of depth; love; and a persistence and critical attitude. These must be employed as we proceed upon another year of the study of Torah, both in the synagogue during services and especially in the various classes in which all of us are called upon to attend.

The rewards are beyond description. At the very least, they will give us a sense of pride, a sense of identity, a sense of sufficiency of the spirit. A learning Jew is not a frightened Jew. Only an ignoramus is always afraid and apprehensive. A learning Jew can take any anti-Semitism in stride; an ignoramus is always seized with panic and hysteria, usually out of proportion to the threat.

Some time ago, I discussed with an uncle the problem of anti-Semitism. I know how American Jews react to it, but I was curious as to the psychology of the Jew who lived all his life in the *shtetl*. This uncle, who has shared in both cultures and both worlds, told me of how when he was a child he was walking with his grandfather, my great-grandfather – the man after whom I am named, and who was known reverently and affectionately in the family by the name of the town where he served as Rav, when they were accosted by a young Polish peasant who hurled at them every foul-mouthed anti-Semitic insult which had become a venerable tradition among both Polish peasants and intellectuals. My uncle, having been exposed to the modern world, was shaken. Yet he noticed that my great-grandfather simply continued, as if nothing at all had ever happened: impassive, unruffled, unconcerned. Said my uncle to my great grandfather, "How come? How can you just continue? Aren't you bothered by all this?" The Rav replied, "What are you talking about? How can I possibly be concerned by the likes of him? Don't you understand? I am a man who has a Torah! A man who has Torah is never concerned by the rantings and the ravings of some semi-ignorant lunatic. The slings and arrows of that kind of fortune can never hurt him."

So let us begin this year with the pride of having the Torah. Let us be people of Torah. Let us never be satisfied with merely hearing the Torah being read on Shabbat. Let us proceed to study it during the week as well. If we are Orthodox Jews, if we are proud Jews, we must be studying Jews.

"For they are the life and the length of our days..." [evening prayers] – because that is what life, certainly Jewish life, is all about.

Three
The Senses of Torah*

ALL TOO OFTEN, WE TEND TO OVER-INTELLECTUALIZE Torah, even in our symbols, as if Jews characteristically suffered from oversized crania. We forget that the Torah addresses itself not only to man's mind, but also to inner man, not only to his intellect but also to his intuition and his instinct, even to his very senses. Torah is concerned not only with man in the objective world, but also with the subjectivity of humans.

Two texts in this regard come to mind, one from today's (seventh day of Passover) Torah reading, and one from tomorrow's (eighth day of Passover) Haftorah, and both of these give us several insights, by use of symbols into Torah and the senses.

In the *haftara* we recite tomorrow, we read of Isaiah's description of the Messiah: "*vahariho beyirat Hashem*" (Isaiah 11:3). The usual English translation is, "And his delight shall be in the fear of the Lord." I do not know what basis there is for this interpretation, unless it is that cited by Rashi, according to which *vahariho* comes from the word *ruaḥ*, spirit. Hence, a more accurate translation would be, "and he shall be inspired by the fear of the Lord."

Kimḥi and Ibn Ezra follow the interpretation quoted by the

---
* April 21, 1976

Talmud (*Sanhedrin* 93b) in the name of Rava. Rava contrasts this clause with the rest of the verse, "And he shall not judge after the sight of his eyes neither decide after the hearing of his ears." The Messiah, as judge, will not avail himself of the senses of sight and sound. These are course, direct, and material – and they can also be deceived. Contrariwise, the sense of smell is less open to deception. It is more subtle, more indirect, more ethereal. Hence, says Rava, *vahariho beyirat Hashem* means that the Messiah's God-fearing quality will endow him with a sharpened sense of smell; *mero'ah vedein*, he will "smell and judge." The Messiah will judge not by sight or by sound, but by smell or aroma. He will have an acutely developed intuition, a highly honed instinctive ability to discern what is right and what is wrong, to distinguish between justice and injustice. Even in colloquial language, we say of someone with sharp intuition that he "has a nose" for what he is doing. So of the Messiah, according to Rava, does Isaiah say that his fear of God will endow him with a divine sense of smell, and an innate capacity to react to right and wrong.

But the Talmud records yet another opinion, that of Rabbi Alexander who states that this verse teaches us that the Messiah was laden down with mitzvot and suffering as heavy as millstones. The word *vahariho* comes not so much from *reiah*, smell, as from *reihayim*, millstones. Rabbi Alexander emphasizes not the sense of odor as much as the tactile sense, the sensitivity to weight. Messiah will find that his good deeds and his suffering are both as heavy as millstones. We are here taught that Torah does not come easy even to the Messiah. So do we often refer to faith in God as "the yoke of the Kingdom of Heaven," and to the commitment to Torah as the yoke of Torah.

The Torah reading of this morning engages yet another one of the senses. After the crossing of the Red Sea and the Song of Triumph, we read that "And they were not able to drink waters from Mara for they were bitter" (Exodus 15:23). The Israelites cried and complained to Moses, and Moses was instructed by the Lord to cast a stick into the waters and the waters became sweet.

What is the significance of this seemingly unimportant detail? The Talmud states that water is a symbol of Torah (*Taanit* 7a). In his book, *Degel Mahaneh Ephraim*, Rav Moshe Hayyim Ephraim comments (Exodus 15:23) that at the times the waters of Torah seem restrictive and inhibiting and even repelling, we must understand that this does not reflect on Torah. Instead, it reflects upon us! Thus, honey is sweet – to any healthy individual. But if one is sick, even honey tastes bitter. So, if Torah appears bitter, it is a symptom of a profound malaise, a disturbing sickness that is our fault, not the fault of Torah. The sweetening of the bitter waters therefore implies the healing of man so that Torah once again tastes sweeter than honey.

Indeed, it was the Baal Shem Tov (the grandfather of this author) who, in his commentary on Torah, commented on this very verse that the antecedent of "for they were bitter," is not the waters, but the Israelites! The Israelites were bitter, and that is why the water did not taste good. Had they been loyal, faithful, sweet, the waters would have tasted sweet too!

Hence, Torah is heavy, but never bitter! We must welcome the idea of Torah as heavy as millstones. Only that which is heavy can be an ennobling discipline. We must be mature enough to have gotten rid of that faddist idea of three or four decades ago, "peace of mind," which really was peace of mindlessness.

Young people today who want easy salvation can get it very cheaply indeed on the streets of this city. They can be approached by salesmen for oriental religions or a thousand other cults who will promise them, for no effort at all, the sun and the moon, and even the Reverend Moon.

However, serious young Jews today are not looking for an easy way out. Those who have any *reiah* at all, any sense of discrimination, any refined intuition, are looking for *reihayim*, for millstones, for a disciplined way of life. I have found that for them the terms *meikil* and *maḥmir*, those who take a more lenient and more stringent view of halakha, are totally irrelevant. They are not looking for forced leniencies and not for artificial stringencies; they want the truth, no matter how heavy it will bear down upon them. Indeed, I have found that the concern as to whether a rabbi is more lenient or more stringent generally is restricted to those over the age of forty! Those under forty are not terribly concerned that a rabbi may be too strict! They are willing to bear any burden, even those of those millstones, as long as they find the results in a meaningful and ordered purpose of life, a life which is sweet, which is not "bitter waters."

I should like to pause for a moment of reflection on a man whose life incorporated these senses of Torah. I refer to my late revered teacher, Dr. Samuel Belkin. Of him it was true that, "He was laden down with good deeds and with suffering as with millstones" (*Kiddushin* 29b). He bore an enormous burden of mitzvot for the congregation of Israel. His was the responsibility for leading and building the greatest Torah institution in the world, as well as a major university. In addition to much personal suffering, the mitzvot themselves were millstones of suffering. He had to put up with opposition, which often was harsh and cynical and unjust. His was the lot of endless worry about the survival of his beloved institution, and the great community which it served and will continue to serve.

It was also true of him that he would "smell and judge." He had a subtlety and an insight that were second to none. There was about him an aroma and atmosphere of genuine humility and greatness at the same time. He often would judge not by his enormously sharp intellect, but by his finely sharpened, intuitive sense of what was right and wrong, appropriate or inappropriate.

And above all, he made Torah sweet. I remember coming to him for the first time in May of 1944 as a young lad frightened, anxious, and nervous, to be orally examined by the President of Yeshiva College in order to determine whether I could qualify. I entered his office, awe-struck. But he engaged me in pleasant and casual conversation which lasted throughout the entire interview. As I left, I was relaxed and happy that this great man had been so easy with me. It was only a day later that I realized that he actually had given me a thorough examination in Talmud, but he had made it so painless for me! How sweet! During the entire time that I attended his Talmud lectures, and for years thereafter, he was to me the epitome of the sweetness of Torah: sweeter than honey and even the honeycomb.

The above is not meant as a eulogy or a panegyric of Dr. Belkin *zt"l*. I mean this, rather, as an illustration of what Torah can and ought mean to us, both individually and collectively.

Torah is a heavy burden, especially in the modern world. But we shall bear it. It grants to its bearers an added more ethereal quality, a more refined *reiaḥ* – a sensitivity to right and wrong, moral and immoral. And it is a spiritual exercise which restores health so that we can appreciate the infinite sweetness of Torah.

For it is important not only that Torah makes sense, but that all our senses be geared to Torah. "All my bones say, O Lord who is like you" (Shabbat morning prayers).

Four
Strange Medicine*

THE BIBLICAL ACCOUNT OF THE REVELATION AT SINAI begins by informing us that it took place during the third month after the Exodus from Egypt: *"baḥodesh hashelishi letzet Bnei Yisrael"* (Exodus 19:1). The Children of Israel left Egypt in the middle of Nisan, and the Torah was revealed to them at the beginning of Sivan.

The rabbis of *Midrash Tanḥuma* (*Parashat Yitro* 10) wondered why God waited all this time before giving the Torah and did not present Israel with the Five Books of Moses immediately upon their leaving the land of their servitude. The touching answer Rabbi Yehuda Bar Shalom gives is couched in warmth and charm. It can be compared, they tell us, to the son of the King who had been very ill. When he recovered from his illness, his father said, in royal indulgence: "I shall wait for three months to give my son the opportunity to recuperate, and only afterwards *olikhenu lebeit harav lilmod Torah*, will I lead him to his teacher in order to have him study Torah." In the same way, when Israel left Egypt, there were amongst them many *baalei mumin*, people who were deformed and crippled because of the oppressive work of Egypt, and therefore the Almighty said: "I will wait until they are completely recovered, and only afterwards will I give them the Torah."

* May 18, 1964

The great Kotzker Rebbe, whose challenging insights are always relevant to every age, asked the following question (*Sneh Bo'er BeKotzk*). In a previous passage, the same *Midrash Tanḥuma* (*Parashat Yitro* 8) quoted approvingly the words of King Solomon in his Proverbs and applied them specifically to Torah: "they shall be healing for your body, and marrow for your bones" (Proverbs 3:8). Now if Torah is considered by the Rabbis as a medicine, as a health-giving substance, then why was it necessary to wait these three months? On the contrary, just *because* Torah is considered a medicine it should have been given immediately, to assist in the spiritual recovery of the Children of Israel. The answer that the Kotzker Rebbe gives is of extreme importance to all of us today. Torah is a medicine, he agrees, but a strange medicine: it works only if the patient knows that he is sick. It is effective only if the patient agrees that something is wrong with him which needs correction. And the situation of the Children of Israel was especially calamitous because they did not even recognize that they were *baalei mumin*, that they had absorbed terrible impurities from the abysmal spiritual climate of Egypt and its slavery. Hence, they had to wait for the third month, for during this time they learned that there was something wrong with them, and only then might Torah be effective as the medicine which would heal them.

So Torah is a strange medicine. Like certain kinds of psychological therapy which are effective only when the patient has attained insight, Torah is effective only if the patient knows that he needs it, that he cannot live without it.

It may have occurred to many of us often to wonder: here we are, having worked so hard and labored so diligently for Torah in this country. Yet, while Orthodoxy has achieved much, we are so very far from our goal! How often we seem at the point of utter frustration.

May I suggest the reason for the lack of proper returns on all our investments of time and energy, of money and worry that the patient – American Jewry – did not know that he was sick! And if the patient thinks that all is well with him, Torah cannot help much. It is a rule in the business world as well: you may have the best product in the world, but if the public feels no demand for it, you cannot sell and stay in business.

May I also suggest that in recent months, or even weeks, something dramatic has occurred which, frightening as it is, gives us new hope that American Jewry now knows its true condition, and hence Torah may yet become the medicine which will save American Jewish life.

No doubt most of us have either heard of or read that sensational and much discussed article in *Look* magazine entitled, "The Vanishing American Jew." The burden of this article was that, considering the progressive assimilation of American Jews into the general environment, particularly as a result of intermarriage, the entire American Jewish community is threatened with gradual extinction. Now, *Look* has been roundly criticized by a number of Jewish leaders and spokesmen for national Jewish organizations. It is true that the gloomy forecast by the magazine may have been exaggerated for the purpose of selling more copies. Also, there is no doubt that the article, appearing in a popular weekly periodical, was not annotated in scholarly fashion and supported by long columns of statistics. Nevertheless, it cannot and ought not be denied that the major contention of the article is unfortunately valid!

Only a few months ago, in a much more profound and well documented article, a major researcher writing in the *American Jewish Yearbook* for 1963 warned that the alarmingly high rate of intermarriage combined with the depressingly low birth rate of American Jews threatened our entire future in this country. Public relations problems aside, I fear that we are confronting the truth in this warning about our future.

Yet I believe that we ought to welcome these reports; not because, according to the article, Orthodoxy is least affected by the plague of intermarriage – that is little consolation for us.

Rather, we ought to welcome this news because of its shock value. Perhaps this will wake up some of our sleeping brethren who slumber in their own little cocoons of official optimism.

We ought to welcome what has now been told to the entire world, because this confirms sadly what we who stand uncompromisingly in the Jewish tradition have been warning our fellow Jews not for three months and not for three years, but for over thirty years – that without Jewish education, without Shabbat, and without mitzvot, the community will surely assimilate and ultimately disappear.

For too long now, ours has been a lonely voice in the wilderness crying out: you will not be able to keep the Jewish people alive and surviving merely on an ethnic basis; a young man or woman with academic training will, if not thoroughly grounded in the total religious experience of Judaism, refuse to accept that it is necessary to continue to be a Jew merely because of nationalistic or racial reasons.

Above all, we welcome this revelation because with this new realistic awareness of our own condition, maybe something will be done. Now that American Jews begin to realize how sick our community is, perhaps we will be ready for the beneficial therapy of that strange medicine called Torah. Perhaps now efforts at teaching Torah to our generations of American Jews will become more effective. Maybe with the growing realization that our community is filled with *baalei mumin*, with those who are sick and deformed for having ignored Judaism, for having decimated its principles and halakha and for having forsaken the heritage of parents and grandparents, maybe with this realization the medicine of Torah will work.

By a remarkable coincidence, this past week has seen another report that is very important. And perhaps those who are weary of statistics will have more faith in the insights of a distinguished American sociologist. Professor Robert MacIver, with whose purposes we totally disagree but whose analysis we accept as valid, addressed the American Council for Judaism on a theme which seemed to bother both him and his hosts: the "continuing alienation" of Jews from the rest of American society. Put in other words, this means that both the good professor and the American Council for Judaism are disturbed at the *slow* rate of assimilation! Whose "fault" is it that we have not assimilated completely at this late stage of American Jewish history? Professor MacIver blames the "distinctiveness of Jewish culture" as expressed in such phenomena as Shabbat, "food taboos" (for which read: kashrut), and the Jewish strictures on intermarriage. He blames, in addition, the idea of separate Jewish schools, i.e. the Jewish day school system, and the tendency to form special Jewish organizations for matters of general interest (probably referring to organizations such as the Association of Orthodox Jewish Scientists).

Is the professor right? Yes, he is! Would that our non-Orthodox Jewish friends listened closely to what he says. He notes well what it is that has saved us to this day. And they are not the solutions that have been offered by our deviationist fellow Jews, whether the half-Reform or quarter-Reform or completely Reform, whether Yiddishists or Hebraists, whether secular Zionists or any others with pet solutions for our problems. No mere "adaptations" can heal the sick heart of American Jewry. Not even fighting an ever-diminishing anti-Semitism with an ever-growing budget, which seems to be the peculiar blessing of our "defense organizations," will accomplish much towards saving American Jewry. Israel is important, Yiddish is important, Hebrew is important, but these alone have not helped and cannot help. At best they are tranquilizers, at worst merely placebos. You cannot treat a serious medical problem with a couple of aspirins!

This we must all recognize – especially those who want to juggle the Jewish destiny, being not completely Jewish, yet not completely non-Jewish; not traditional Jews, yet not assimilated Jews. In the long run, this is an impossible task, doomed to failure. Now we must recognize not only that we are sick, but that there are certain forces that have kept us alive and well, and that we must do all that we can to reinforce those healthy elements: Shabbat, kashrut, the ban against intermarriage and inter-dating, and above all education, and more education! Perhaps, to take up the hints of Professor MacIver, there should be Sabbath-observing young Jewish professionals who will form organizations for social workers and lawyers, for architects and behavioral scientists, equivalent to that of the Association of Orthodox Jewish Scientists. Above all else, it is time that we recognized our spiritual illness and our need for Torah. Then, and only then, will Torah become, as Solomon put it, "healing for our body and marrow for our bones." If these revelations will shock American Jewry to an awareness of its own impoverished spiritual condition, then our timeless message will become more effective than it ever was before. Then all of us will begin to build more day schools. Then we shall begin to emphasize more Hebrew day schools on the high school level. And let us take a leaf from the book of our Catholic friends who now realize that high school and college education is religiously far more significant than elementary school education. Then we shall begin, as a community, to pay more attention to Yeshiva University.

Then, above all, we will begin to devote more attention as well to Jewish youth on campuses throughout this country. There are in our country, at present, some three hundred thousand Jewish college students, representing about 75% of the college age youth of the Jewish community. In a short time, this is expected to rise to 90%. Now there is an organization by the name of Hillel which is devoted to the welfare of the Jewish student. But the solution we have in mind is more than what most Hillel groups do or can offer. What we mean is Torah and the study of Torah above all else. It is therefore an indication of the new opportunities opened to us to learn that a group like Yavneh, which started out only about five years ago with a handful of students at Columbia University, has now spread to about seventeen campuses throughout the country and in the short space of five years now numbers some twelve-hundred students who, in order to belong to this organization, must undertake a regular program of Jewish study for which no college credit is offered! Imagine if Yavneh were given the proper support by the adult community, they might today number not eleven hundred but perhaps eleven thousand members!

In summary, then, this new realization of how far we have gone downhill may make us ready to return and climb once again to the summit of Sinai. We have achieved, to use the words of the Midrash, the *ad shetashuv nafsho min haḥoli* (*Midrash Tanḥuma, Parashat Yitro* 10). We have recuperated enough to appreciate how sick we were. Now is the time to take the next step: *olikhenu lebeit harav lilmod Torah*, the return to the house of the teacher to study Torah!

Now is the time when we can achieve greatness, when every effort can produce unprecedented results. It is in dedication to this kind of commitment that we turn our thoughts to the past, entertaining memories of devoted parents and teachers, and promise to consecrate ourselves to a greater, brighter, and holier future for us, our children, and all Israel.

Five
The Arrogance of Modernism*

ON THIS PLEASANT FESTIVAL, I BEG YOUR INDULGENCE for sharing with you a sense of irritation. I am allergic to the word "modern." I am incensed at the smug and complacent *am haaretz* who says to me, "How can you be Orthodox when you are so modern? How can you refrain from smoking or driving on Shabbat or eating non-kosher food, how can you fast on Yom Kippur, in this twentieth century?"

I am similarly upset when I hear people saying, "He is religious, but modern," in almost exactly the same tone as one would say, "He is slightly insane, but sincere," as if modernity can save the benighted religious soul from the damnation to which the unsophisticated are foredoomed.

I even confess that I am uncomfortable with the title "Modern Orthodox." There is an arrogance about this assertion of modernity which should give offense to any intelligent and sensitive man. There is no better term that I have found, but I flinch when I articulate the words.

Modernity – what conceit! How vain, how meaningless! As if the accident of being born into the space age makes one

* May 23, 1969

superior to the past, because "we" know so much more than those of previous generations did. But who is this "we" who know so much? If any of us has advanced knowledge in any one specialized field, does that give us warrant for feeling better and greater than ancients whose wisdom often ranged far and wide, whose interests were universal? Because we have the ability, through no fault of our own, to turn a knob on the television set and watch a spaceship near the moon, does that make us better than Newton or Kepler or any of the other geniuses of the past who discovered and described the laws of the universe which have made our age possible?

I am moved to speak of this theme because Shavuot is the anniversary of the giving of Torah, and an old Torah it is! It is *not* a modern Torah. It is a holy Torah, a powerful and wise and meaningful and vital and just Torah, but no, not a modern one. It is not materialistic or hedonistic or youth-oriented or secularistic or "with it."

Judaism maintains that truth does not depend on time. The Maharal of Prague observed that the festival of Shavuot, unlike all the others, is not appointed by the Torah to a special date on the calendar. It is only indirectly fixed as seven weeks after Passover. Why is this so? Because, answers the Maharal, Torah is beyond time (*Derashot HaMaharal* p. 24). Its truth is not a function of the age in which it was given. Jews, therefore, should not assent to what Jacques Maritain has called "chronolatry," the worship of what is latest in time.

Every age is, of course, modern in its own eyes. But the tendency to consider this modernity as a virtue is fairly recent. I believe that it is largely the result of a misinterpretation of evolutionary theory: since life is supposed to evolve to higher forms, therefore I am greater than my father, and he was greater than his... Thus, one might conclude, and many often do, that the religious tradition that comes to us from the remote past is inadequate for us, because the ancients were not modern and we are.

This feeling afflicts even profoundly religious people. About 150 years ago, the Protestant theologian Friedrich Schleiermacher wrote a book entitled *On Religion: To Its Cultured Despisers.* How revealing! Those who despise religion are modern, they are cultured. We are benighted, we are behind the times. So it is with most religious folk, we labor under the heavy burden of an inferiority feeling because we are not modern.

I do not mean to say all that is modern is bad, and that as an observant Jew I am against modernity. That would be as absurd a notion as the supposition that all that is modern is good and true. Over 200 years ago, Lord Chesterfield wrote: "Speak of the moderns without contempt, and of the ancients without idolatry; judge them all by their merits, and not by their age" (*Letters to His Son*, Volume 25, p.52).

I admit that it sometimes seems as though the rabbis of the Talmud were inclined to ascribe greater virtue to ages past: "If those of the earlier generations were the children of angels, we are merely the children of men; and if they were but the children of men, then we are like mules" (*Shabbat* 112b). But I do not think that this implies a *general* condemnation of later generations. It is not really anti-modernist. Rather, it represents a specific judgment that they made when comparing their own generation with that of the Prophets, and I agree that spiritually we have been in decline for a long time.

But that does not mean that in their view, human history *always* deteriorates. On Shavuot, the farmer who would bring his *bikkurim*, or first fruits, would recite the passage that begins: "My father was a wandering Syrian" (Deuteronomy 26:5). Abraham had very humble origins (*Rashbam, Deuteronomy* 26:5). And on Passover, we proclaim: "Once upon a time our ancestors were miserable idol-worshippers" (Pesach Haggada). The past is not always better than the present. And, by the same token, the present is seen as leading to a much greater future: the coming of the Messiah.

Nevertheless, Judaism does not subscribe to "chronolatry."

We must not submit to the arrogance of modernity. This modern worship of modernity results in a number of patent absurdities. Consider this: if we are bright and intelligent and wise because we are modern, and therefore superior to past generations, how will we be judged by the coming generations? And how will they be judged by the ones following them? And if by their standards we are primitive, how sure are we now that we are right in anything we believe, including our arrogant assumption about modernity?

Even our vocabulary suffers and reveals the foolishness of making a fetish of modernity. The very word "modern" has become shopworn. Many people have begun to use "contemporary" instead. More recently, learned journals have featured a spate of articles on the "post-modern." What is to come next? Post contemporary? Post-post-modern?

It is true, generally, that technological knowledge and ability is cumulative and that every generation is, in this sense, greater than the one preceding it. But it is not necessarily true in ethics and morality, in religion and in the life of the spirit. And even technologically, the idea of constant and uninterrupted progress is true *only* provided that there is no devastating war that results from technology itself, so that man is reduced, as Albert Einstein put it, to fighting the next one with bow and arrow; and provided that the flow of technical knowledge does not become so vast, so enormous, so stifling, that mankind strangles on it, unable to digest and use it.

But to repeat, whatever may be true of technology and science is not necessarily true for religion. Love and hate, fear and reverence, the sense of mystery and worship, all these are independent of artifacts and gadgets and mathematics. Science and technology make us more effective, but to what end? Modern scholarship is more critical, but are we wiser? We have great communications, but do we say more that is worth saying? We can have more fun, but are we happier?

Torah is not anchored to the "modernity" of any age. For

Shavuot is not given a date in the Torah. The Torah given on Shavuot is beyond time. It applies to then and now and to tomorrow. It is always "modern" and yet never merely "modern."

I recently read with amused contempt a report of the Jewish Telegraphic Agency which is pertinent to the idea we are discussing. It tells of a statement by a Reconstructionist leader who urged that Jewish community centers remain open on the Sabbath to serve "the needs of those who do not hold to Orthodoxy." He also declared that the Sabbath "must be re-established not as a restrictive day of fourth-century worship and rest, but rather as a twentieth-century turn-on to relevance."

What colossal *am haaratzut* for a "rabbi" to speak so disparagingly and *unknowingly* of fourth-century Judaism, the very high point of the creation of the Talmud! It is difficult to find a more apt illustration of the "arrogance of modernity," arrogance and *ḥutzpah* and immaturity! Not even a supposedly religious teacher, but any cultured individual, would refrain from such obvious vulgarity in preaching "relevance." So the Shabbat should not be a day of worship and rest, but a "turn-on to relevance!" What does that mean? Are we to abandon the synagogue and repair to the gymnasium? To quit our services and head for swimming pool? To spend all Shabbat on election campaigns? On breaking windows on the campus? In demonstrations?

"Turn-on!" I would recommend instead a simple "turn," or as it is known in Hebrew, *teshuva*, or repentance. That may be less "exciting" and less "modern," but it would lead to more humility and respect and responsibility.

No, Torah is not geared to the calendar. It does not tell us that we have to be modern and always accord with the *zeitgeist*, with the spirit of the time. The late Dr. Raphael Gold once made this comment: Adam and Eve, after they sinned and corrupted their lives, heard the voice of the Lord: "And they heard the voice of the Lord God walking in the garden *leruaḥ hayom*"

(Genesis 3:8), which is usually translated as "toward the cool of the day," but which may just as well be translated, "according to the spirit of the day." Once they had sinned, they approached God only according to the *zeitgeist*, according to the canons of modernity. It is the way and the wages of sin: man attempts to reduce the infinity of God to his own pitifully puny dimensions. He turns away from God, and "turns on to relevance." He breathes deeply of the *ruaḥ hayom* and, intoxicated, becomes arrogantly and vulgarly "modern."

So let us not be frightened by the word "modern." Let us not be awed by the self-satisfied ignoramuses who feel superior because of the accident of their birth in this generation. *The Jewish Chronicle* may criticize us, and *Commentary* may not like us. The rich and the powerful may consider us antiquated. But that is no tragedy, it is not fatal. We shall survive – long enough to have to put up with yet another generation which will consider the present moderns as outdated as we are supposed to be! Modern science and technology and culture have contributed much that is of abiding value for mankind, just as they have failed miserably in so many other areas.

What we hold to be true, we hold to be timeless, unaffected by the years, and uncorroded by the ages. We hold our Torah to be true; it is a *Torat emet*. And Torah and truth are both timeless, even as God, the *Noten HaTorah*, is beyond the ravages of time. What is true is valuable, even if ancient; and what is false remains contemptible, even if modern and up-to-date.

In the closing words of the *Akdamut* prayer, which we read this morning, we recited the following words: "Exalted is the Lord from the beginning of time to the end, who loved us and was pleased with us and gave us His Torah."

Six
A Premature Obituary and an Immature Religion*

JEWISH TRADITION MAINTAINS THAT THE SIN OF THE Golden Calf, which we read in today's portion, is a recurring sin of which most generations to some extent are guilty. It is important, therefore, to understand it and its causes and see whether it is germane to this generation's problems.

The sin of the Golden Calf is usually thought of as symbol of greed. This is not true since its creation was volunteered by Israelites who donated their own personal effects for it. If anything, it was not motivated by greed, but by a lopsided scale of values where gold is given first priority – in our estimation of others, in our hopes and dreams and aspirations and prayers, in other words, in our religion.

What causes this? The Torah merely tells us that Israel thought that Moses was unduly late in coming down Mount Sinai with the Ten Commandments, *"ki boshesh,* that Moses had delayed in descending the mountain" (Exodus 32:1) and so they directed Aaron to make for them a god to lead them through wilderness.

---

* March 12, 1955. This chapter was reconstructed from Rabbi Lamm's bullet format.

The comments of our Rabbis are of great interest and extremely pertinent here. They say that a rumor spread through camp that *"Moshe met,* Moses is dead!" (*Shabbat* 89a). In our own terms, Judaism is done for, it has no future, it is a thing of the past. In almost the same words, Nietzsche had Zarathustra clamor, "The gods are dead," and in almost the same tone, modern deviationists from Torah maintain that, for all practical purpose, Judaism, as we've known it throughout ages, is dead.

What gave cause to these expressions of hopelessness in Judaism, to this death-knell sounded for Torah? Why are people convinced that Orthodoxy cannot survive? The causes are the same as those that gave rise in the desert camp of the Children of Israel that *Moshe met,* the ugly premature obituary of Moses.

One reason for the birth of this rumor was the fact that Satan had cast a pall of black darkness all about the mountain. Lost was all its primitive beauty, the glory of Mount Sinai which only a short while ago was a breathtaking scene of *Matan Torah.* It was now only a dark, dimly lit, poorly lighted little mountain. One of reasons people cheerfully sound a death-knell for Torah is, therefore, the *social-esthetic* one. The shul is not bright enough. It is not as pretty as the gilded temples. They must have something more attractive, to glitter and glisten, to show our non-Jewish neighbors the beauty of our temples. To show what we can accomplish and attract the socially prominent of our own people. This attitude maintains that a religion which is not pretty is not vital. It is too dark; it's unhandsome.

The second reason is a *personal* one. Satan had projected an image of Moses on his deathbed floating high above the people. This exemplified their attitude that religion is too far above us, that it has no relation to us, and that Torah is irrelevant in modern times. It talks about such impersonal things as the Sabbath and prayer and love of God and love of neighbor, but doesn't hold solutions for my daily problems. It's floating in the stratosphere, but we need something to *come down to our level*. When Torah is considered that high above, that unconnected with our dances and card-parties and social aspirations and business worries, then *Moshe met*, it's gone and done for.

The third reason is an *intellectual* one. The Rabbis say to read *ki boshesh* to mean *bashesh*, that he's already six hours late. This expresses the attitude that Orthodox Judaism has "missed the boat," it's outmoded. It's "behind the times" and isn't up-to-date with latest intellectual currents. It wants to turn the clock backwards. *Moshe met*, if it's not up to date, then it's as good as dead.

Imagine the chagrin and embarrassment of the hasty obituary writers when Moses reappeared and they saw him standing there at foot of mountain, out of the darkness, on earth, and on time. And there, by his very presence he answers their questions and belies his reported death:

As his face shines with the *karnei hahod*, he seems to say to them that the outer glitter is nothing; it is the inner light which counts. And if you think that Torah is not clothed beautifully enough, then your task is to make it so, to build beautiful, well-lit shuls, not to build pagan gold-gods.

If you think that religion is too high, that it is too beyond you, and is too impersonal, then try to reach up, try to grasp for it; lift yourself up to it. Do not bring it down to your low level. And second, look closely at that image, and you'll realize that its height and distance is only a foolish mirage, that it is actually close to you, it is near to you. Sabbath is the essence of your relationship with nature – organic and mute – every moment of life. Prayer is the yearning of your innermost self, which sometimes you don't even know. Kashrut is there to teach you to be a man who is self-controlled and disciplined, not an overgrown boy.

Finally, don't foolishly think it is late, that the Torah is "behind the times." It is *beyond* the times, and so can never grow old. With Torah, time is not the matter of a calendar, but of eternity. Hitch your Religion on to the latest intellectual fads, and it is self-destroyed in few years. The Reform latched itself to Neo-Kantianism; now that it is outmoded, so is Reform. It teamed up with nineteenth-century progressivism; now both are "behind times." Conservatism, particularly its leftist expression called Reconstructionism, is based exclusively on Dewey and instrumentalism; now it is slipping into the backwash of intellectual history, soon to be completely out of vogue. Orthodoxy, or better, Torah Judaism, can absorb all these trends, use them and even strengthen them. But it can never base itself on them to the detriment of Torah itself. Torah is "up-to-date" only with God, who is above time, and therefore Torah has eternal validity. Torah is not subject to time's ravaging effects on ideas which are only temporal.

When the obituaries are announced, and the people say "*kum asei lanu elohim*, make us a god" (Exodus 32:1) – let us fashion out a religion with our own hands, let us bow to our own images, let's get ourselves a man-made god instead of believing in the God-made Man – then it is a danger sign that a people is on the brink of great destruction and strife.

Today as then, the Golden Calves will be ground to dust. Today as then, Moses will reappear in the form of a revitalized Torah Judaism. The hasty arguments versus Torah will be seen in all their ludicrous falseness. And with the disintegration of the gods of gold, a grateful Jewry will dutifully return to God, away from immature religion based on primitive obituaries.

May that day come soon, and God willing it will. For already we have begun to witness the first signs of a serious return from the gilded gods to the God of Torah. Already we've seen Orthodoxy presented in beauty, inner and outer. We have seen people understand it in their most personal aspects life. We have seen those closest to contemporary scientific and philosophical thought remain loyal to Torah. And may God willingly reaccept his children, without strife, without plague, but with love and with blessing.

Seven
Why Moral People Need Torah*

A FUNDAMENTAL OF JUDAISM THAT IS A PERPETUAL source of wonderment is the relation of religion and morality. A major part of Torah concerns the social and ethical obligations of man to his fellow man. The question is, why should it be necessary to have revelation at all for ideas and regulations of behavior that man can arrive at independently? Do we not know of societies preceding that of Israel at Sinai which arrived at moral codes by themselves? Do we not know individuals who are not committed to Torah and who nevertheless lead ethical, decent lives?

The question is too extensive and the problem is too significant to attempt anything approaching an exhaustive answer. But on this festival of revelation, permit me to commend one specific line of approach.

The site of the revelation is called by two names in the Bible: Sinai and Horeb. The Rabbis, as is their wont, offer us a remarkable insight by means of a play on words. They took these two names of this mountain where the Torah was revealed and related them to two rather negative terms. Sinai

---

* June 11, 1970

is reminiscent of *sina*, hatred, and Horeb to *ḥurva*, destruction. Essentially, what they mean to say is that Torah, revealed at Sinai-Horeb, is what allows man to avoid hatred and curtail destruction in the world.

Simply put, the Rabbis meant that the Torah is, as Zvi Kolitz has called it, "the great deterrent" against the innate evil that rises from the breast of man. Torah restrains him, it curbs his evil propensities, it allows man to repress his concupiscence and envy by accepting the moral code of revelation.

However, just as Judaism acknowledged man's evil inclination, so it posited his native moral intuition. Man is, after all, created in the image of God, and just as God is good, so does man possess extensive reservoirs of goodness and morality. Man naturally possesses noble wishes, the feel for ethical living. Men are good and virtuous on their own, even without divine instruction.

Why then is Torah necessary? It is needed because it contributes the setting, the structure, the context for moral life. It takes man's disparate and fragmented moral inclinations, and unifies and integrates them into an overall pattern of living.

This is necessary – and this, I believe, is the major import of the Rabbis' play on words – because there is nothing quite as dangerous as virtues on the loose, ideals gone wild, ungrounded goodness. Without the structure and the grounding provided by Torah, virtues can turn venomous, ideals can devour us, goodness can strangle us. Never before has any generation realized as does ours that moral perfectionism can turn nihilistic and threaten us with total destruction.

What the Rabbis implied is that without Sinai we are at the mercy of *sina* and without Horeb we are at the mercy of *ḥurva*, all wished upon us by ungrounded virtues. We need Torah not only to curb our *yetzer hara*, but also to direct the *yetzer hatov*, lest it become a Frankenstein's monster and turn upon us.

Here are but a few immediate examples of how a virtue, overdone, can undo us.

Honesty is, everyone will agree, a great ideal. But honesty can sometimes shade into uninhibited frankness, and frankness is often used as a tool to humiliate another person, with total insensitivity to his feelings. Honesty, then, can be used as a weapon to crush another human being. The person who honestly tells you what he thinks of you, and in the process demolishes your ego, has taken a virtue and, because it is ungrounded in anything deeper and more transcendent, allowed it to become an instrument of evil design.

Consistency is another such example. Certainly, consistency is a desideratum. But consistency can lead to rigidity, to immovability, to an unwillingness to change for the better: since I already made a statement or performed an act, I feel that my future conduct must be mortgaged to consistency with my past.

Humility, one of the greatest of all virtues, can prove a source of *ḥurva*. If I feel totally humble and lacking in importance, then I yield to the feeling of impotence with regard to improving myself or bettering my society. I then lose my self-respect. And a man who has no respect for himself can have no respect for others. Hence, *sina*, hatred.

How does Torah solve the problem? How does Sinai impede *sina* and Horeb avoid *ḥurva*?

Each virtue or ideal, by and of itself, can be destructive if it follows a straight line of development. Great ideals carried too far are usually counteractive. But within the context of Torah, within a total religious situation, where moral principles issue from one source and give man the feeling of responsibility to that source, there takes place what might be called a dialectical motion: each virtue is checked and modified by an opposite virtue, and both blend into a third ideal that preserves the best of both. In this manner, all of man's life is integrated, unified, elevated.

Consider the following illustrations and we shall see how individual virtues can lead to *sina* and *ḥurva*, whereas if they are integrated dialectically in the context of Sinai and Horeb, they add up to a *Torat ḥayim*, to a living Torah.

Idealism is a superb phenomenon. But it also can be deadly. Idealism sometimes morphs into ideology – idealism in rigor mortis, accompanied by excessive zeal, which turns into blind passion and ends up as fanaticism. This is the way of *ḥurva*, destruction.

Realism alone, a virtue usually professed by those of middle age and over, is certainly a virtue for people seriously attempting to construct the good society. But realism alone usually turns into resignation, the acceptance of evil and corruption, and this gradually becomes reaction, and finally cynicism. This is the way of *sina*.

However, when each reacts upon the other, when each modifies the other, when a man has the combination of idealism and realism as a result of his anchorage in Sinai-Horeb, he then has avoided the pitfalls of hatred and destruction.

Freedom is certainly one of the noblest ideals of man. Yet, freedom taken to an extreme is utterly destructive. If everyone will "do his thing" without recourse to a transcendent Judge and without concern for his fellow man, there can be no constructive life. Personally, it leads to immorality, and socially it leads to anarchy. This is the way of *ḥurva*.

Its opposite is responsibility. But responsibility can be taken to an extreme, too. People who feel overly responsible for everyone and everything, live under a crushing burden. All of existence becomes joyless, and they begin to lose spontaneity and therefore initiative. People who are constantly oppressed by the burden of responsibility, by the guilt feelings that it engenders, hate life. This is the way of *sina*.

We have many such examples of each element taken to an extreme by itself. The freedom of parents to crush prenatal life, which now seems to be in vogue, will eventually lead to utter destruction, because it is only a small leap of logic from feticide to infanticide, to getting rid of infants who may not fulfill our ideals of mental and physical health, or, eventually, ethnic and genetic respectability. The opposite can also be oppressive and bring hatred and animosity into life: an absolute decision that never must the life of a fetus be taken. Halakha combines freedom and responsibility and offers us guidelines as to when the one should be exercised, when the other. When freedom and responsibility react upon each other and with each other, dialectically, we have attained the moral maturity of Judaism.

Reason or intellect has always been accorded the greatest respect in both the Jewish and Western traditions. Yet, by themselves, they make life insufferable. In our own days they have resulted in the passion for research, harsh and cruel technology, the depersonalization of society, the fostering of inhumanity. Parents and children are strangers to each other, husband and wife barely know each other, teachers and students are related to each other as employer and employee or even worse. This is the way of *sina*, hatred.

Reason must be merged with emotion. But emotional experience and expression alone are also inadequate. The New Romanticism of the campus has tried to correct the balance by reintroducing into American life the validity of sentiment, feeling, heart. But it has tended to ignore the element of intellect; it has tended to downgrade the role of the academy as a meeting place of ideas and criticisms. And so, this New Romanticism and celebration of emotion and sentiment have turned into hysteria, to a clash of blind passions, the way of *ḥurva*, destruction. When we take these two ideals together, and allow them to play upon each other and modify each other, then we have the *adam hashalem*, the "whole man" of Jewish tradition.

The same might be said for love and discipline. Love by itself can lead, amongst equals, to promiscuity, and from parents to children to what has been called "smother love," to a warping of the child's personality. It is the way of *ḥurva*. Discipline alone leads to rigidity, to a lack of warmth and affection in family and society, to a sense of isolation and alienation by the individual who feels crushed in his loneliness. It is the way of *sina* or hatred. Together they lead to the fullness of Jewish life, to the interplay of *din* and *rahamim*, justice and mercy, which is the reflection in human society of the attributes we notice in God.

As a last example, we might take the tendency to look to the past and the one to look to the future. There are those who, especially in Jewish life, seem fixed upon the past. Their entire Jewish expression is one long *Yizkor*. But this is the counsel of despair, it reflects a sense of unhappiness and even *sina* towards conditions that prevail today. The other extreme is that of ignoring the past and acting as if we can create Jewish life *de novo*, all from a fresh beginning, looking only to the future and ignoring our roots. This is foolish. It is the way of *hurva*, or destruction. A true Jewish attitude requires consideration of the past and looking to the future at the same time. To drive on the highway of life, according to Jewish teaching, we must keep our eyes on the road ahead but every now and then, regularly, look at the rear-view mirror to know where we have come from.

It is worth repeating what I have said before from this pulpit – anything worthwhile is really worth repeating occasionally – in the name of the great Kotzker Rebbe. He said: "*Klug iz krum*," intelligence can sometimes lead to crookedness, as intellect is abused for corrupt ends. "*Gut iz ni'uf*," goodness can sometimes lead to immorality, when out of sheer love one consents to demands that are immoral. "*Frum iz shlecht*," piety can sometimes be malicious, when it is expressed as self-righteousness and intolerance. "*Aber gut un klug un frum, das iz a Yid*," when you combine these virtues of goodness and cleverness and piety, then you have the whole Jew.

All that we have said on revelation as the unifying factor in the moral life, on Torah as the undergirding and transcendental stabilizing factor of virtue, we can find in a famous passage in the Book of Ruth. When Boaz first makes the acquaintance of Ruth, he blesses her in the following words: "May the Lord recompense your work, and may your reward be complete from the Lord the God of Israel, under whose wings you have come to take refuge" (Ruth 2:12).

The Malbim asks: is not this verse repetitious? The first half and the second repeat each other – the Lord recompense your work, may your reward be complete.

No, answers the Malbim, there is no redundancy here; each expression means something different. *Pa'olekh* and *maskurtekh* are rewards for different kinds of activities. *Pa'olekh* is the wages of the *po'el*, the artisan, whereas *maskurtekh* is the salary of the *sakhir*, the day laborer. The *po'el* (artisan) is one who is paid for piece work, he is compensated only for what he achieves, no matter how long it takes him or how little time he spends on it. The *sakhir*, however, is paid not for achievement of specific tasks, but for the time he spends in his labors, whether it be an hour, a day, a week, a month, or a year.

What Boaz said to Ruth is this: may God compensate you for your work as a *po'el*. Before you accepted the Revelation of Sinai-Horeb, whilst you were yet outside the community of Israel, you were a highly moral person, one who was ethically gifted. Everything you accomplished that was noble and decent will receive its reward from God. But you will be compensated as a *po'el*, only for what you achieved that was deserving and noble. But you lacked an overall pattern; your life was moral, but only in its individual expressions, not as a totality. Now, however, that you have come to rest under the wings of God, that you have accepted the Torah of Sinai-Horeb, all your life is integrated in the service of God, every moment is lived under this great commitment to the Covenant. Now God judges the overall pattern of your life, He sees how your virtues blend and mesh and merge, and He considers not your individual acts alone, but their totality – you are a *sakhir*, and your reward will be great and complete, not only when you are actively engaged in particular moral missions, but in their totality. As a Jew and the heir of the Sinaitic tradition, your reward is *shelema*, whole, as you have come to place your entire life in all its aspects under "His wings."

Without Torah, without Revelation, we can have at most *pa'olekh*, moral credit for individual deeds, and, at worst, the ravages of *sina* and *ḥurva*, hatred and destruction.

Let us rededicate ourselves on this Shavuot, once again, to the great Covenant of Sinai, the great heritage of Horeb, so that not only will the Lord recompense our work, but that our reward, our *maskoret*, be complete and whole before the Lord God of Israel.

Eight
The Other Revelation*

IT IS WELL KNOWN THAT SHAVUOT COMMEMORATES God's self-revelation, His giving of the Torah at Sinai. It is less well known that another revelation took place at the same time – that of Israel to God! The response of Israel, in accepting the Torah, that too was a revelation. If *Matan Torah* (the giving of the Torah) is God's revelation, then *kabalat haTorah* (the receiving of the Torah) is Israel's revelation to Him.

God's revelation is a question of theology; man's revelation is a matter of religion. Today, let us speak of that other revelation, the revelation of man or of Israel.

Hasidim tell the following story. The Baal Shem Tov told a number of his Hasidim that he would take them along to Berditchev in order to visit a very great saint, Rabbi Liber the Great. When they came to his home in Berditchev, they did not find him. Whereupon they went to the market to seek him. From afar, they noticed that he was deep in conversation with what looked like an ordinary peasant. The Baal Shem Tov did not allow his followers to disturb Rabbi Liber because, he explained, the peasant was really Elijah the Prophet, in disguise. (There is a long history in the Jewish tradition of revelations of Elijah to saintly people). The Hasidim were amazed: how wonderful to

* June 6, 1973

behold Rabbi Liber in the process of experiencing a revelation of Elijah! But the Baal Shem Tov told them differently: it is not Rabbi Liber who has the privilege to have a revelation of Elijah, but Elijah who is privileged to have a revelation of Rabbi Liber!

The late Professor Heschel (who cites this story in his *The Earth Is the Lord's*) points out that in the same sense, Hasidism as such was a sudden revelation of Jewish holiness which had been accumulating for centuries. This kind of revelation is the most important of all!

Our theme, then, is that the receiving of the Torah is as great as the giving of the Torah; that the response of "we shall do and we shall obey" is as extraordinary as the revelation of God in "I am the Lord, your God." If to God's revelation we reacted with the exclamation "Who is like You among the gods, O Lord," then to our revelation, He responds, "Who is like Your people Israel, one nation upon the earth."

If such a human revelation were to take place today, what would our society have to show for itself in its self-revelation? I believe the answer is a rather mixed bag. The most salient feature of our civilization, in almost all of its aspects, is that of technology, the advance in the use of tools. Technology has allowed us to enhance health, education, abundance, and convenience. Yet, it has often given us the means for more efficient mass murder. It is a rather moot question as to whether technology is good or bad; it is neither. It is what we do with it that tells us something about our moral character.

The Center for Science in the Public Interest has recently written that "there are more scientists developing fruit-flavored deodorant sprays than new methods for detecting birth defects. More engineers are involved in electronic eavesdropping than in preparing 'child-proof' caps for hazardous house-hold chemicals. More talent is being used for color television and bigger bombs than in increasing food production and investigating the side effects of insecticides."

There is nothing wrong with the "neutral" use of technology which enhances the conveniences of man. But when we so ignore the urgent needs of man for survival and health in favor of goals that are destructive of his life, spirit, and environment, then we are revealing a major feature of our civilization's character: the misuse of technology.

What, on this Shavuot, do we reveal as Jews? Here too the reaction must be mixed.

For one thing, we ought to be satisfied that in our days we have experienced the reassertion of ethnic pride. There is still plenty of embarrassment that some Jews experience because of their Jewishness in the world today. But most of the younger generation no longer tries to "pass," whether they have decided so for and by themselves, learned it from our African American neighbors, or gleaned it from the general winds blowing in the world today. They are no longer embarrassed by and ashamed of their Jewishness.

Does world Jewry reveal divisiveness in its intragroup relationships? Certainly, it is true that there is much controversy in our midst. But I do not believe that that is a major feature of Jewry in our times. Indeed, from a historical perspective, one may say that there is more unity today than there has been in most periods of Jewish history. The spectacular feeling of oneness that took place at the giving of the Torah – as Rashi (Exodus 19:2) comments on the singular "and he [Israel] camped there," that Israel was "like one man with one heart" – have rarely reappeared in our long history. Since the brothers sold Joseph into slavery, that act of hostility has been more characteristic of our communal life than the unity achieved at Sinai.

So, I am pleased that today we can mention to our own credit that there is a large degree of mutual Jewish concern, such as the concern of American Jewry for Israel; of Israel for Soviet Jewry, opening up its arms and homes and purses; and the worry of all of us for the remaining Jews in Syria and Iraq.

As a people, at the Festival of Revelation, we can be fairly happy with our gains.

Of course, the great negative feature of our lives is the question of our religious and spiritual continuity. And here we must accept it not only as a national but primarily as a personal challenge to each and every one of us.

As individuals, Shavuot asks us what we are ready to show as we reveal ourselves to God: whether we possess an inner life, loyalty, commitment, a pattern of conduct which we are prepared and proud to reveal – or ashamed to expose.

I suspect that most of us, if we are honest, are not quite ready for this "other revelation."

And yet, on a deeper level, the revelation of ourselves to God must be based upon another revelation – the revelation of ourselves to ourselves!

And here, the Jewish tradition, especially the Hasidic one, has a great deal to teach us. Thus, the author of the *Tanya*, the father of Chabad Hasidism, interpreted prayer as – revelation. Normally, we consider Torah as revelation, yet R. Shneour Zalman tells us that all of prayer is revelation – from ourselves to ourselves: it brings, from the depths of our subconscious to the level of our awareness, the inner divinity, the spark of God that lies dormant within us, the image of God that is immanent in us.

I spent last Saturday at a unique American institution, Camp Brandeis near Los Angeles, California. It is an adult version of the NCSY or YUSVY seminars that have been so popular in the East for our teenage children. It affords Jewish adults, singles or couples, an elementary exposure to Judaism, with information and experience, in a manner that will hopefully keep them going and encourage them to deepen and intensify their Jewish identity, concern, and commitment.

What were they doing there? I asked myself. Here are people who, for the most part, were far-out Reform, unaffiliated, or assimilated. Some of them told me that not only did they not have a bar mitzva, but that neither they nor their parents were married with *chuppa* and *kiddushin* by a rabbi in the traditional or religious manner. And so I wondered, what were such alienated Jews doing, spending a whole weekend listening intensely to an Orthodox rabbi taking a "hard line" on such matters as belief in personal God, a personal Messiah, "who is a Jew," study of Torah, and, above all, loyalty to halakha? I discovered the answer. They were revealing themselves to themselves! And it was the first step in revealing themselves to God.

It is interesting. I tried to impart as much inspiration and information as I could in the several addresses I gave this weekend. But of all the things I said and taught, I was amazed that they were most responsive to the following message:

I see in you alienated, searching, inquiring, but hesitant Jews – true fear of God. No, not "fear of God" in the sense that an observant Jew means it, that is, awe, reverence, and piety; rather, I see in you true, genuine, *literal* fear! I detect in you that you are afraid – afraid of committing yourselves, afraid of the consequences and implications of accepting a new life. Most of all, I suspect that you fear that you do not have what it takes to be genuinely religious, to relate to God, to respond to Torah, to do the Jewish thing. So let me repeat to you a tale that the Rabbis tell in the Talmud that may make you feel more comfortable.

Before a man is born, the Talmud (Nida 30b) teaches, while he is yet a fetus in his mother's womb, he is not alone. He is always accompanied by an angel, and the angel teaches him all of Torah. But the moment before birth, the angel puts its forefingers across the lips of the child and makes him swear that he will forget all that he has learned, and so the child comes into the world innocent of all knowledge of Torah.

What do they mean? Once we know how to read the Rabbis, it is fairly simple. They mean to tell us that although we come to Torah without any knowledge of it consciously, we have already absorbed it fully in the very structure of our personality. The study of Torah is not the grafting of alien knowledge on a neutral mind; rather, all study of Torah is a matter of relearning, recollection, of remembering that which had been forgotten. It means that Torah and the Jews really conform to each other, they are appropriate to each other, they articulate with each other. Hence, you can respond, because inwardly or naturally you already correspond!

Their search, their response, was a revelation to me. It was a revelation to them. I hope that on this Shavuot of revelation, it was a wonderful, happy revelation to our Father in Heaven.

The great mystic, Rabbi Isaac Luria, once said that the giving of the Torah somehow makes up for the sin of Adam (Adam Yashar p.224). Now, I am sure that the great Kabbalist had profound and esoteric thoughts in mind. But permit me to give his statement my own non-mystical interpretation.

When God called out to Adam, "Where are you?" (Genesis 3:9), when He asked him to give an account of himself, to say once and for all who he was, what he was, what he desired, where he was going, Adam remained silent. As he later explained: "and I was afraid because I was naked and so I hid" (Genesis 3:10). Adam revealed nothing because, realizing his spiritual nakedness, he was afraid that any self-revelation would be a case of indecent exposure.

But at Sinai, when God revealed Himself in the words "I am the Lord, your God" (Exodus 20:2), Israel, though recognizing its failures and deficiencies and inadequacies, its own spiritual nakedness, responded with love, "We shall do and we shall obey" (Exodus 24:7). It was a revelation of its willingness to clothe its spiritual nakedness with the words of Torah, to cover its bare head with the crown of Torah.

In this way, the giving of the Torah made up the for the sin of Adam; the self-revelation at Sinai atoned for the non-revelation in Eden.

On this Shavuot, may we – as nation and as a community, as families and individuals – reveal to our Father in Heaven the dimension of greatness and spiritual beauty which will be a revelation, even to ourselves.

Nine
The Age of Gemini*

ON THIS SHAVUOT, THE COMMEMORATION OF *MATAN Torah*, the covenant at Sinai between God and Israel, I want to speak about two aspects of the Torah covenant, both for their intrinsic value and because they are relevant to the state of Judaism in the State of Israel today.

It is no secret that polarization in Israel on religious questions becomes sharper each day and that the incipient signs of a *Kulturkampf* are already with us. The nature of the Jewish religion and Judaism's conception of the nature of the State are, therefore, very much germane not only to this holiday but to these times as well.

My first point is this: the purpose of Torah is neither some kind of arbitrary spiritual exercise, nor the beating of man into submission in order to aggrandize the divine ego. Rather, Torah is the divine instrument for man's spiritual welfare and fulfillment. The Torah is God's formula for man's moral development. The prescriptions may be difficult, they may entail discipline and renunciation, but the purpose of Torah and the commandments is the good of mankind. Our Rabbis meant this when they said (*Berakhot* 25b): "Torah was given not for the ministering angels." Rather, "the commandments were given

* May 30, 1971

in order to purify and enlighten man's character." "It is because God wanted to endow Israel with extra privilege that He gave them the Torah and the commandments."

Human concern as the core of Torah is implied as well in a charming Midrash, in which the Rabbis speak somewhat parabolically and make use of the signs of the Zodiac. They did not mean to wish upon us a belief in astrology – though that would be quite contemporary! – but rather they used the *mazalot* or Zodiac signs as symbolic representations. Why, ask the Rabbis in *Pesikta Rabbati* (*piska* 20) was the Torah given during this month of Sivan and not in other months, such as Nisan or Iyar which precede it? They answer with a parable: Once there was a king who had a beautiful daughter whom he loved very much. When he succeeded in making an appropriate match for the princess, he called his counselors together to discuss with them the proper wedding arrangements. One advisor said, "Let the princess be seated atop the greatest elephant in the realm and there, high up in a golden booth, let her be led to and from the wedding procession." Said the second nobleman, "The elephant may indeed be tall, but it is essentially an ugly beast. Better than that, let the princess be seated on the handsomest horse in the realm, and on that elegant steed let her be seen by all your subjects." The third counselor, however, objected to both plans. "Yes," he said, "the elephant is tall and the horse is handsome, but neither of them has hands to clap or feet to dance with, and they have no mouth with which to sing and praise the beauty of the bride. Therefore, it is more fitting that the bride be borne aloft on the shoulders of the guests (somewhat as is done in contemporary Hasidic weddings!) where her own people will be able to sing and dance and clap for the princess."

Similarly, the Torah was not given in Nisan or Iyar, for the symbols of these months are non-human: the Zodiac sign for Nisan is the ram, Aries, and the sign for Iyar is the ox, Taurus. The appropriate time for the giving of Torah is neither of these, nor any of the other months of the year, but only that one month in which humans appear: the sign of Sivan is twins, Gemini. The Torah is not too tall for us, it is not too beautiful and sublime for us. Rather than being beyond us, it was made for us, for humans who can respond to it with song and praise and devotion and enthusiasm.

For us Jews, the great age is not the Age of Aquarius, but the Age of Gemini. Torah is a celebration of man as a being worthy of divine concern and divine covenanting. This is something that Torah authorities must always keep in mind and, indeed, have always kept in mind. This is evident to anyone acquainted, for instance, with the great responsa literature on the *agunah* problem. Halakhic authorities have always responded with enormous consideration and sympathy for those who were disadvantaged by the Law. Today there are other issues of *ishut* (marriage or divorce law) which are paramount in the public forum in the State of Israel. This congregation is acquainted with these problems from reading the press, and there is no need to detail them. Let me, however, mention but this: it is all too easy to criticize the Israeli rabbinate and lay all blame at its feet. But bear in mind that the Rabbis of Israel are confronted by extraordinary difficulties. Rabbis did not invent the law, and they cannot abrogate it at will. They have a freedom of interpretation, but the halakha is not infinitely plastic. The law is not a rubber nose that can be pinched and shaped and formed at will. No rabbinate worthy of its name and its tradition can allow itself to be bullied. And the press in Israel is so hostile to the rabbinate, that one need but pick up any issue of *Haaretz* and, before opening it, he already feels the vibrations of antagonism and even hatred. The government has arrogated to itself the right to dictate to the rabbinate decisions of law. But just as there is a limit to the religious involvement in politics, so is there a limit to the political intrusion into halakha. With all honor and tribute, genuinely meant, to two great national heroes, Prime Minister Meir and General Dayan, they have yet to prove their credentials as scholars of halakha before they may dictate how a religious law shall be decided.

Yet, at the same time, we must concede that it is true that certain insensitive zealots have compounded the problems almost beyond repair, zealots for whom such unfortunate scandals are balm for their sick hearts, who act as if the identification and exposure of *mamzerim* constitutes some kind of mitzva, whereas in truth such vigilante activity goes against the whole ethical spirit of the Sages. Such unconscionable zealots do exert a pressure, and it must be resisted by the proper and authorized interpreters of Torah, given in Sivan, the month of Gemini – Torah, whose major concern is to enhance the humanity of its communicants. We must intensify the search for more lenient and permissive interpretations of the halakha, the limits of which have not yet been reached. However, such genuine and sympathetic interpretations cannot be attained and the search cannot be enhanced by this unceasing press campaign and by an attempt at a government *diktat* to the rabbinate – and also not by those for whom the Torah was given exclusively to the ministering angels and not to man, who have forgotten that Torah is the month of Gemini, of humans.

My second point is that Torah was given to us not only as individuals but as a people. Israel accepted the Torah as an *am*, as a nation, as a responsible collectivity. They signed, as it were, to the contract called Torah as a corporate individual.

One of the most profound historians of Jewish religion, Yehezkel Kaufmann, has written in his epochal *Toledot HaEmunah HaYisraelit*, that the great ḥiddush or uniqueness of the Sinai Covenant was not so much its content, for much of that content pre-dated Sinai; a great deal of it was known, even according to tradition, to Abraham and his descendants, and some of it was the common possession of all civilized humanity. Its major contribution was that this moral and religious law was not directed by a group of sages or by edict of the king to various individuals, but was revealed by prophecy as a covenant to an entire people; it was an agreement made by God, through prophets, with a *nation* as such. And Israel is responsible to this Covenant *as* a nation.

Thus it is that at the end of his days, Moses refers to the Covenant of Torah as having been sealed not only with "those who stand with us here today," but also "for those who are not here this day."(Deuteronomy 29:15) Individuals can obligate only themselves; when a nation obligates itself, it includes its whole timeless entity – the dead and the unborn as well as the presently living. Therefore, when Israel covenanted with God at Sinai, it included us in that obligation as well. We are included in the responsibility of the Sinai Covenant by virtue of our being Jews, hence part of a nation.

So we may understand why the reaffirmation of this Covenant took place at specific times in Jewish history. The first Covenant was given to Abraham as the founder of the people, and then at Sinai through Moses when, for the first time, Israel itself was covenanted as a nation. There are at least three other mentions of confirmation of this Covenant: immediately before entering Canaan; after the conquest of Canaan in Shechem; and the confirmation of the Covenant that will take place after the redemption, as mentioned by Jeremiah.

Why are these reaffirmations necessary, since the original Covenant still holds? Are not the laws and principles of the Torah eternal, and if so, why is it necessary to again swear allegiance to the Covenant?

I suggest the following answer: at critical junctures in Jewish history, there hung over our people the threat of its dissolution as a nation, as a separate corporate entity. Were such fragmentation to come about, it would spell the abrogation of the covenant, for the covenant was made not with individual Jews, but with Israel as a people. So, before entering Canaan, in which the tribes which heretofore had traveled through the desert together would separate to their respective territories, bringing on the threat of decentralization and hence fragmentization, it was necessary to affirm the Covenant as a people. After the conquest of Canaan at Shechem, when some of the tribes were to stay on one side of the Jordan and the others were ready to disperse in their various assigned areas, the threat of tribalization was even greater. Had this tribalization taken place, the Covenant would have been vitiated. Hence, it had to be reconfirmed.

This important lesson must not be forgotten by the secularists of Israel. Secularism is not identical with agnosticism. Rather, it aims at the privatization of religion, it preaches the idea that a man's religion is his own business and neither state nor society can have any interest in it. Indeed, the reason for the sensitivity of Orthodox Jews to the "Who is a Jew?" question is precisely this attempt to separate religion from nationhood. This secularization, appropriate as it might be for other religions, cannot be applied to Judaism, for which it becomes a kind of Christianization of Judaism, a Protestantization of Torah. But this cannot be, for Judaism is the religion of the Covenant, and the Covenant was made with Israel as a people, not as a collection of diverse persons.

Hence, we may understand why the prophet Jeremiah (chapter 31) speaks of a new covenant, *berit ḥadasha*, in the days to come. It is the same Torah to which we will reobligate ourselves – "I will place My Torah within them..."; but what will be reemphasized is the nationhood of Israel as one of the covenanting parties: "I shall be for them for a God, and they shall be for Me a *nation*." (Leviticus 26:12). It is almost as if the prophet were speaking of and to our own days. Israel is not just an ethnic continuation of an ancient civilization, but God's people, the *Am Hashem*! Today, the threat of fragmentization is not that of tribalization, but that of secularization – and it is just as real.

So we learn two lessons on Shavuot, this commemoration of *Matan Torah*. The first is that the revelation of Torah on this month of Sivan represents the human element, the Age of Gemini, the twins. The second is that the Torah was given to Israel as a nation.

The sign of Sivan is twins. Perhaps, in terms of our discussion, we may say that each Jew has a double or "twin" relation to the Covenant; as an individual who must choose, and as a member of the Jewish people which is chosen. Each Jew is an autonomous person who volunteers his service, and is also a member of the people who covenanted with God and therefore is precommitted and preobligated. We are each Gemini: an independent individual and an integral part of the people of Israel.

Woe to him who is a Jew only by birth, only ethnically. He is chosen against his will, pulled and dragged kicking and screaming into the covenanted peoplehood and its sacred history. Such a Jew has a split personality, one whose individuality is in violent conflict with his membership of the Jewish people.

Happy is he who, born a Jew and therefore obligated by the Covenant of over 3,500 years ago, yet turns about and freely chooses to love and to live Torah conscientiously. He is whole, and the twins are as one; his selfhood and his Jewishness are united.

Such a man is worthy of Sivan, and he helps to usher in, to a dehumanized and depersonalized world, the renewed Age of Gemini.

Ten
Judaism as an Alternative*

IN A WELL-KNOWN PASSAGE, THE *MEKHILTA* (*YITRO parasha* 5) relates that the Holy One offered the Torah to the various nations of antiquity, but that all of them rejected it because of various objections they raised to certain of its precepts. Then He offered the Torah to Israel, and Israel accepted it with alacrity.

Now this is more than an interesting legend, spiced with a dash of Jewish pride. It is the Rabbis' way of emphasizing the revolutionary character of Torah, and especially the Decalogue. The Torah, they meant to say, was given not to confirm standard ideas and prevailing prejudices, but to challenge and change them. The Ten Commandments were meant to teach a religion with a difference, to offer the world an alternative to the colorful but lifeless paganism in which it was immersed, and that that alternative was seized by Israel.

To us, in our age, the Decalogue often seems to be a commonplace. Yet consider how radically new it was in its own day. To a society that practiced paganism and fetishism, the Torah declared "You shalt not make for yourself a graven image" (Exodus 20:4). To a world which accepted slavery as normal and in which even the free man was doomed to a life of drudgery, the

* January 23, 1965

Bible proclaimed the law of the Sabbath, and commanded rest even for the man-servant and woman-servant. And to a civilization which entertained the conception of man as a thing, to be used and exploited, and in which, therefore, old parents who could no longer be gainfully employed were abandoned and discarded as excess baggage, the Decalogue declared, "Honor your father and your mother" (Exodus 20:12), even if you can no longer obtain any benefit from them. Maimonides considers this differentness of Judaism a fundamental of Torah. Part III of his *Guide for the Perplexed* (from chapter 26) teaches the proposition that whereas Torah did not attempt to diverge from the world so radically that it could not be followed by ordinary men, still the mitzvot take exception to the mores of the masses and to popular platitudes, and emphasize those ideals and ideas wherein we differ from the rest of the world. To Maimonides, one of the major purposes of Jewish life and Jewish law is the verse "you shall not walk in their statutes" (Leviticus 18:3). This is not meant, assuredly, to preach the doctrine that the Jew be different just for the sake of contrariness, but rather to offer the world an alternative to its standards, its slogans, and its sanctified biases.

Indeed, one of the great lights of the Mussar movements of nineteenth-century Lithuania, Rabbi Simcha Zissel of Kelm, discovered the same idea in the salient features which Judaism ascribes to each of the three patriarchs. In the Jewish tradition we identify Abraham with the trait of *ḥesed*, love and kindness; Isaac with the quality of *paḥad*, fear or reverence; and Jacob with the characteristic of *emet*, truth and integrity. Certainly each of them possessed many virtues. Why, then, were these three chosen above all others? Because, Rabbi Simcha Zissel tells us, each emphasized specifically those themes which were most neglected by his contemporaries; he attempted thereby to correct the ethical imbalance in the surrounding culture. Abraham lived in a society dominated by Sodom, one characterized by cruelty and pitilessness and heartlessness;

therefore, he championed the quality of *hesed*, of goodness and decency and charity.

Isaac dwelt amongst the Philistines, about whom he was moved to say that "there is no fear of God in this place" (Genesis 20:12). Therefore, he dedicated his life to highlighting precisely that quality which they lacked: *pahad*, a feeling of reverence and the fear of God. Jacob was involved most of his life with his uncle and father-in-law, Laban, who achieved unparalleled notoriety as the great deceiver and thief. Therefore, his chief concern was to represent *emet*, truth and honor and integrity.

All the patriarchs, therefore, preached their principles despite popular perversions. All of them understood that whereas you must live in history and in the world, nevertheless, in order to enhance the moral and spiritual health of all of society, you may not downgrade your differences with the world, disguise your uniqueness, or play down your own peculiar principles. Hence, where cruelty is acceptable, we opt for *hesed* or pity; where wild abandon reigns, we Jews choose *pahad*, a sense of awe and reverence; where deceit is common, the Jew strives for *emet*, truth above all.

During the last fifty years or so, traditional Judaism in the Western world has expended much effort to prove that we are not really that different from others; that we can and do acculturate and adjust and speak the language and the cultural idiom of Western civilization. That is as it should be; had we not done so, we would have lost much more than we did.

Yet we must now return to our original and main function: to offer an alternative to the world; to speak the word of God in the great spiritual abyss; to remain critical of the local idolatries that desecrate every generation. Now that Orthodox Judaism has, to an extent, become naturalized, we must turn our energies to offering Jewish alternatives to the great world problems. We must speak the authentic word of Torah on the great issues of our day – fearlessly, courageously, and honestly.

How does Judaism offer such options or choices to modern

men? As illustrations, let us consider how three of our religious institutions do indeed offer alternatives to mid-twentieth century man.

We live in an age of almost total mechanization and increasing automation. The machine has become our master, and we have become slaves to the gadgets, beholden to the time-clock and telephone, even as our children are glued to that one-eyed monster called the television set. Our futures are settled for us by uncanny computers which ravenously swallow vast amounts of statistics, only to disgorge omniscient little prophecies about how long we shall live, what we shall eat, where we shall move, and how we shall vote. It is a world that is terribly cold and impersonal and inhospitable.

What a marvelous relief, what a fabulous alternative, the Shabbat is! And if indeed the Shabbat is warm and personal, full of Jewish charm and humaneness, it is because it offers us an alternative; at least one day where we do not push buttons, we do not manipulate implements, we are not at the mercy of electrical discharges, and we do not engage in travel, which, inwardly, we do not want to do anyway! A person has time for his family and for himself. Once upon a time we used to commend the Shabbat because on that day the Jew received a *neshama yetera*, an "additional soul." Today, however, it is sufficient to recommend the Shabbat merely because on that day, unlike all others, a man has a *neshama*, a soul! During the entire week, caught up in the gears and gadgets of our complex and impersonal society, man feels that he lacks a self, that he has become reduced to a mere thing. On Shabbat, therefore, he rises above his mechanized and automated environment and he reacquires a soul, a *neshama*.

The study of Torah, as any knowledgeable Jew knows, is the greatest of all Jewish commandments. Yet what we often do not realize is that the study of Torah, unlike the study of any other intellectual discipline, is not geared merely to amassing facts. In Torah, as Rabbi Hayyim of Volozhin pointed out, it is not the *acquisition of knowledge* that counts, but rather, *the act of study*. How important that is for contemporary man! There was a time when we passionately pursued leisure and imagined that society would be transformed into Utopia when we would attain a greater degree of leisure. Now that we are on the threshold of achieving this dream, we view it with dread. Social thinkers are frightened and apprehensive at the advent of the shorter work week and earlier retirement combined with greater longevity. What shall we do? How shall we spend all this time that we have suddenly obtained?

Judaism, however, has no need to invent new "projects." The purpose of life, according to traditional Judaism, is the study of Torah – the act of study, the process of learning, the time we spend engaged in the pursuit of Torah. If our children are trained from their earliest youth in the idea that Torah must be studied for its own sake, not merely in order to recite a *haftara* at their bar mitzva or to impress one's elders, that study is its own excuse and reason, they will continue in this pursuit every available moment. Do we not say every day in our evening prayers concerning Torah, *"ki hem hayeinu ve'orekh yameinu,"* that the words of our Torah are our life and the length of our days? Indeed, the purpose of our existence, our very lives, is Torah: *ki hem hayeinu*. More than that, when we have discharged our active business or professional duties, which we regard as merely necessary preliminaries to a life of leisure, then we can devote all our days to the pursuit of Torah, for this Torah is *orekh yameinu,* the length of our days!

The Jewish principle of *tzniut*, of modesty, represents an urgent option for modern man, a crucial alternative for the degradations of our lust-inundated and sex-obsessed world which has obliterated the boundaries between love and lechery. The Jewish standards of morality in its fullness, from the requirement of *mehitza* to the practice of *taharat hamishpaha*, are not the moral criteria of the majority of our culture, not even those of the majority of Jews today! We take strong exception to the prevailing standards. Any true Jew is revolted by the well-phrased libertinism and licentiousness which sullies the undergraduate newspapers of some of our greatest universities, *including some that are Jewish-sponsored and Jewish-supported*! We cannot, must not, shall not, consent to a situation which gets progressively worse, in which sex has become the debased coin of the realm, and which is expressed in the modern American pagan's supreme commandment "thou shall do whatever your heart desires." We shall continue to protest the kind of perversion which regards chastity as "square" and considers a "well-rounded character" one that has indulged in illicit experiences. The Jewish principles of purity are not nearly as popular as the cheap promiscuity that has become fashionable. But we were brought into this world to offer alternatives not palliatives!

Such insights abound in Jewish tradition. What we have mentioned are but a few illustrations. Far more work must yet be done. For those willing to invest their time, devotion, knowledge, and skill, there are as yet undiscovered treasures within the Jewish tradition. Labors of love by many people are required in order to elucidate for us the uniquely Jewish approaches to such questions as: business ethics in the changing industrial and managerial structures; the role of women; the exciting discoveries of modern biology and astrophysics; the nature of man and freedom of the will, in the light of new psychologies; the meaning of the Holocaust and the question of theodicy; the State of Israel – a non-Messianic, independent Jewish state; the relation with ethical non-believers and religious dissent in a world of cultural pluralism. There are issues so new that they have not been named yet; and some problems that, because they are timeless, deserve to be taken as fresh and serious challenges to modern Jews to ferret out new but genuinely Jewish alternatives to the old answers. Scholars have before them years of dedicated labor in the great mine of Jewish tradition to identify for us the jewels of Jewish thought, and polish them so as to enlighten mankind with Jewish alternatives on the great issues that are the concern of a world in crisis. These insights can illuminate all peoples; these alternatives can redeem a humanity struggling to survive. And all Jews, whether or not they are scholars, can practice the precept of Torah which possesses, implicitly, the most precious wisdom of our faith.

May all of us return wholeheartedly to that Torah of whose giving three and a half millennia ago we read, and which in effect we reaccepted this morning. May we re-echo the sublime response of our ancestors "we shall do and we shall understand." Even as we have determined to "do," to practice Judaism, so may the Almighty endow us with the wisdom of *venishma* – to appreciate its meaning and its relevance, so that we may in turn offer it as a saving alternative and a cherished choice to a confused and distracted humanity.

Then the Torah will indeed become, as it was meant to be, *samma dehayye* (Shabbat 88b), "an elixir of life" – for us, for all Israel, and for all mankind.

Eleven
Orthodoxy and Fundmentalism*

IN THE LEXICON OF RELIGIOUS POLEMICS OF THIS decade, a place of special distinction must be accorded to a relative newcomer: "Fundamentalism." Once upon a time, this word merely denoted a certain Christian sect. Today, however, it is fashionable to use this particular word in order to defame Orthodox Judaism. Anti-Orthodox controversialists, tiring of such dated clichés as "old-fashioned," "reactionary," and "behind the times," have taken to "Fundamentalist" as a fresh and sophisticated epithet which sounds as elegant as it is supposedly devastating. Let an Orthodox Jewish leader express dissent from the cherished dogma of current Jewish bourgeoisie liberalism, and he is dismissed with a wave of the hand: "Why, that is Fundamentalist!" To my dismay, I find that even some of my Orthodox colleagues to the left of me have a tendency to apply the term pejoratively to some of our brethren to the right of us.

Now, if the use of this term is meant to indicate that we Orthodox Jews take our Judaism seriously; that we are vitally concerned with our commitments and loyalties, then we plead

* February 17, 1968

guilty to the charge – and with great pride. But if by "Fundamentalism" is meant what Fundamentalism really was, as a religious movement and spiritual orientation, then it simply is not true. The phrase may be fashionable, but it is flippant and false.

Fundamentalism was originally a sixteenth-century Protestant sect which accepted the Bible as literally true in every single word, and considered the written word, strictly construed as the exclusive religious authority. It recognized no possibility of metaphor, no chance for a deeper-than-literal sense to the scriptural text, and denied the existence of any tradition of interpretation of the written Bible.

Were there ever any such opinions in Judaism? Yes, there were. Two thousand years ago, there were the Sadducees who accepted only the Written Torah. In the Middle Ages there arose the Karaites, a name which derives from the Hebrew *mikra*, Scripture, and which designates a movement which views the Bible in its literal sense as the sole authority of Judaism, to the exclusion of any oral tradition. But the whole of traditional Judaism is against Karaism. Our Judaism was at one time involved in a life-and-death struggle against Karaism, and our survival bespeaks our opposition to and triumph over this movement. We do *not* necessarily accept every word of Scripture in its literal signification. Furthermore, we read the Bible, the Written Torah, only through the eyes of the Talmud, the Oral Torah.

For instance, Scripture tells us that if one man injures another and removes his eye, then his punishment is *"ayin taḥat ayin* – an eye for an eye" (Leviticus 24:20). Taking that verse literally, this would imply that we must physically remove the eye of the man who committed the tort. However, the Oral Law interprets that phrase to mean not physical removal of the organ, but compensation, a payment equivalent to the value of the eye. Furthermore, the Rabbis tell us that in three places, the halakha, which is the essence of the Oral Law, *explicitly* opposes the plain sense of the Scripture: *hahalakha hofekhet et hamikra* (*Sotah* 16a).

So Orthodox Judaism is anything but Fundamentalist! Of course, this does not mean that we reduce all of Torah to a very fine and noble religious heritage from which we may choose according to our taste. We by no means mean to imply an eclectic approach to Judaism, whereby we may accept anything which appeals to us end reject that which, according to our momentary whim, does not seem to accord with contemporary cultural prejudices. What we do mean to say is that the Oral Law is the only interpretation we accept of the Written Law, that halakha predominates, and therefore we are not Fundamentalists at all.

Now, there is one consequence of the non-Fundamentalism of Orthodox Judaism that is not overly obvious. It is a principle that is a bit subtle, but extremely vital to a proper understanding of Judaism. That is, that in Fundamentalism there is a feeling that the mitzva describes an absolute quality of the world itself, the objective material universe, whereas Judaism holds that the mitzva is directed to man, as a subjective discipline, and is not a description of the objective world. Were I to express the same concept in halakhic terminology, I would say that in an ultimate sense all the *issurim*, prohibitions of the Bible, relate to *gavra* rather than *ḥeftza*, to men rather than to objects.

For instance, the Torah prohibits *shaatnez*, the mixing of wool and linen. The Fundamentalist would not only accept this literally – in this case, we do too – but insist that the *shaatnez* is itself an abhorrent object, that somehow it possesses a quality of evil that makes it repulsive. Whereas Judaism considers that this *shaatnez* in and of itself is no different from any other textile or garment, it is *we* who are called to the divine discipline by refraining from wearing a garment made of *shaatnez*. (Indeed, were there anything indigenously evil about a mixture of wool and linen, we would be prohibited not only from wearing it, but also from preparing such a mixture.)

It is for this reason that Rav declares, in a passage cited in the Midrash (*Genesis Rabba* 44:1) that in essence, the laws of kosher slaughtering have no innate significance insofar as the meat itself is concerned: "*Vekhi ma ikhpat li shohet min hatzavar o misheshoheit min ha'oref*, what difference does it make if we slaughter by slitting the throat (which is the kosher method), or kill the animal by breaking its neck [assuming that both methods are equally painless]? *Lo nitnu mitzvot ela litzrof bahen et haberiyot*, the Commandments were given only to purify thereby the human being who observes them." The mitzva, then, does not tell us that certain objects in the world are better or worse than other objects. Inanimate things are neither good nor evil; it is man who becomes good or evil depending upon how he responds to the divine command.

Even better illustrations are offered to us by a distinguished lady in the Talmud (*Hullin* 109b). Yalta, the wife of Rabbi Nahman, observed to her husband, "*Kol ma de'asar lan rahmana, shara lan kavatei*, whatever the Torah has forbidden to us, it also permitted us something similar." For instance, to cite some of the examples cited by Yalta, the Torah forbade the consumption of blood, yet it permitted the eating of the liver, an organ which is so filled with blood that it can never be emptied of its contents; or, the Torah forbade eating the flesh of the *hazir*, but it permitted eating *moha deshivuta*, the brains of a certain fish, which tastes just like the meat of the hog; or, the Torah forbade *basar behalav*, eating milk and meat together, yet it permitted us to eat the *kehal*, the udder of the cow even if it was cooked together with its milk content. In all these cases, we see that the Torah did not imply any innate obnoxiousness of any particular object, or its taste, but rather it directed its remarks at man, at the Jew, addressing his subjective response to the divine command. No object in the world is absolutely reprehensible. There is no taboo or magic with which the Torah is concerned. It is the human being who must submit to God's will. The Jew should not recoil in horror from an object that is forbidden by the Torah, but he should be taken aback at his own weakness when he begins to lose his self-control. There is nothing wrong with *tarfut* as such; there is everything wrong with those who eat *tarfut*. There is nothing wrong with *ḥillul Shabbat*; there is something terribly the matter with those who are *meḥalelei Shabbat*. That is why the Oral Law points out exceptions to rules, exceptions sanctified by the Torah itself.

In a remarkable passage, the Zohar locates the same idea in the Ten Commandments themselves, of which we read in today's portion which describes the revelation at Sinai. Let us take two of the examples offered by the Zohar: *lo tirtzaḥ* and *lo tignov*, the prohibitions against murder and stealing. Ordinarily we accept these as absolute prohibitions. Yet the Zohar teaches us that that is not so. The Zohar points to the cantillations, the musical notes which so often teach us a great deal about the meaning of a verse. Under the word *lo* in each of these two commandments, the note is a *tipḥa*, which serves as a kind of comma, as if the Torah said to us: *lo, tirtzaḥ* and *lo, tignov* – you shall not – kill! and you shall not – steal! How strange! You shall not kill, and you shall not steal; but sometimes: kill and steal!

Yet that is just what the Zohar maintains is the judgment of Torah. Even the prohibition against killing is not absolute; sometimes we must take a human life! As an example, the Zohar mentions capital punishment. Now, it is true that the tendency of the Jewish tradition by and large is to minimize the instances deserving capital punishment, but not to eliminate them completely. As an Orthodox Jew, I have long been in favor of the movement to restrict capital punishment to all but a very few instances, but not to remove it completely from the law books. Thus, I was unquestionably in favor of the hanging of Eichmann when he was captured by Israel. That is why, as an Orthodox Jew, I can applaud the humane sentiments of the ex-governor of Maryland who this week came out publicly for doing away with capital punishment; but I cannot agree with him that it should be done away with altogether. I would keep it for such unusually heinous crimes as genocide or mass murder. That is why too, I can appreciate his lofty instincts when he maintains that life and death are only of the Lord and man may therefore not condemn a fellow man to death – but I do not agree with him. The Torah has told us that there are times when the power over life and death is given by God to the human court, provided that it acts with justice and righteousness. Our reason for restricting capital punishment is not the idea that man never has the right to take life – that is what the Zohar means when it emphasizes the *tipḥa* under the word *lo tirtzaḥ*, – but because of the possibility of a mistake and the murder of an innocent man. To use other examples, in addition to the one quoted by the Zohar, one may cite self-defense, where we are not only permitted but required to defend our lives and the lives of our family by killing one who threatens our lives. Similarly, this would include the right and the duty to bear arms for one's country when it is under attack, for this is the concept of *milḥemet mitzva*. It is Judaism that gave the world its highest and noblest expression of universal peace, but Jews do not embrace pacifism. Our ultimate goal remains always that of *shalom*; but under conditions as they exist now, we cannot ask any human being or any country unilaterally to declare for peace even at the expense of his or its own survival. We accept the Torah absolutely – including the fact that the Torah did not legislate absolute principles without exception.

Of course, it should be clear that we do not mean that it is we who make the exceptions to the Torah's laws, that we play the game of religion by making up our own rules; rather, that the Torah itself, as a "Torah of life," saw fit to state general principles and then to state the exceptions as well.

The second example the Zohar offers is that of "*lo tignov*, you shall not steal." Here too the Zohar finds exceptions implied in the general statement, as if the "you shall not" and the "steal" are sometimes separated. What does this mean? In the Jewish tradition, the concept of stealing is broadened beyond that of taking material objects which belong to someone else. It includes the concept of *genevat daat*, stealing the mind or the knowledge or the confidence or the awareness of another person. Therefore, *lo tignov* means not only to steal material things, but also to deceive or delude another person. Yet, the Zohar tells us, at times it is not only permissible but mandatory to deceive another human being. For instance, if a judge has before him witnesses who are technically valid, but he knows by a sure instinct that they are perjurers and they may condemn another man to death or other form of suffering, he is duty bound by the law to conduct a vigorous cross-examination, and in fact to be devious and deceiving in the course of this examination, in order to expose any conspiracy by the witnesses, should they be false, and thus save the life of an innocent defendant. The same might be said, in addition to the example cited by the Zohar, of a man who is hungry and finds his children starving, and is prevented by the laws of the country from receiving any form of sustenance – who can blame him for stealing?

This principle holds true not only for Torah or religious law in a narrow sense, but for law in general, including the secular and civil law as well. Just as a mitzva has as its purpose the advancement of the relations between man and God, so the civil law is made to ensure the progress of society. Therefore, just as the Torah is non-Fundamentalist and legislates exceptional, so must the laws of the country.

In a broader sense, this means that while law must be respected if society is to survive, at the same time we must recognize that there are times when lawlessness has some justification; or, if not justification then at the very least it is sometimes deserving of our sympathy and understanding. That is why I feel that in the current public outcry against lawlessness that has overtaken our country in recent years and months, we must discriminate between the various kinds of disobedience of the law. I believe, therefore, that we ought to condemn severely and unreservedly the lawlessness of certain unions which seek to choke the entire community by extortion and blackmail. There is no excuse for such conduct by a union, as part of community (the labor segment of society) which has, in concord with other parts of our pluralistic society, come to an agreement as to laws which are just for all, and which now rejects those very laws in order to grab a bigger share of the economic pie. At the same time, I would denounce, but with much less conviction and much less passion and much less certainty, the lawlessness of those elements in our society who protest the foreign military adventures of our country. I do not excuse them; our laws are the laws of a democratic society, and they must be respected. But where citizens genuinely feel that the law requires them to deny their consciences and pervert their own moral stature, then I certainly do not put them in the same category with a union which is lawless for a profit motive.

Similarly, I would denounce without qualification hooligans who take advantage of the civil strife and social unrest of our decade in order to rob and steal and plunder and rape and murder. But I would look with much more compassion upon those minority groups in our country, be they African American or Hispanic or any others, who feel that they have no recourse but to exercise certain kinds of civil disobedience. I believe that such groups have not exhausted all legitimate means to air their grievances. I think we ought to counsel them to have patience, although that is much easier for us who have already arrived at the other side of the social fence. We must recognize that law has often disadvantaged these groups, that the law of the country is made by man and must be changed by man to correct deficiencies in the social structure, and therefore my condemnation of their lawlessness carries with it less self-righteousness, less vehemence, less heat, and perhaps a bit more light. It means that we have got to improve our laws, in addition to using force in stopping lawlessness. Otherwise we encourage the disadvantaged groups in society to come to the conclusion already anticipated in the bitter pessimism of Kohelet, "in the place of judgment [or law], there you will find evil" (Ecclesiastes 3:16).

Two such basic commandments, such as the prohibitions against murder and stealing, according to the Zohar, have a built-in exception. Certainly, this is not a Fundamentalist interpretation. One must add, however, that even this rule, that all rules have exceptions – this too has an exception! The Zohar (*Parashat Yitro* 93b) tells us that the ninth commandment is absolute: *lo taane bere'akha ed shaker*, you shall not bear false witness against your neighbor. Here, the first two words of the commandment are marked by the musical notes *merkha* and *tipha*, which means that they are connected: as if it were written, "You shall *never* testify falsely against a neighbor." The creation of a "credibility gap" by spreading falsehoods is always inexcusable.

Judaism, therefore, is certainly not Fundamentalist – in any sense, except the sense that our conviction and our commitment are unshakeable. For we have two Torahs, not one Torah. And we consider the Written Torah, the *Torah shebikhtav*, as understandable and authoritative only by means of the Oral Torah, the *Torah shebe'al peh*. We are not Bible-centered literalists. We are people of *Torah shebe'al peh*, which is the Word of God as His divine norms are applied to ever new situations.

In the introduction to the giving of the Torah and the Ten Commandments, the *parasha* tells us: *"Moshe yedaber, vehaElokim yaanenu bekol*, Moses would speak, and God would answer him with a voice" (Exodus 19:19). The Netziv tells us that this verse has special significance. It means that not only the Ten Commandments and the Written Torah came from God through Moses, but the Oral Law as well, that which *Moshe yedaber* – which Moses spoke – as well as that which he wrote. This Oral Law too issues from the Almighty; it is uttered not only by the voice of Moses, but *vehaElokim yaanenu bekol*, its force and authority derive from God Himself.

Note that phrase "*Moshe yedaber*" is written in the future, not in the past; "Moses will speak" not "Moses did speak." Not only did Moses once speak to the Children of Israel a long time ago, but he shall speak, always, whenever Jews loyal to the Torah of Moses study or enact the mitzvot contained therein, for then they carry on the dialogue of Moses with God.

And when we do so, and when we confirm our loyalty to both Torahs, the Written and the Oral, the Almighty answers us "with a voice," with the strength to carry on and proclaim the message of Judaism, which is the message of God to an as yet unredeemed world.

Twelve
A Step Backwards in the Right Direction*

THIS SERMON IS OCCASIONED BY TWO FACTORS: A) THE eternal appeal of the Ten Commandments to all people – the entire Western world, and even, or perhaps especially, those who least observe them; and b) a comment made to me the other day, which I am sure is indicative of a large body of unstudied and unlearned and misinformed opinion, to the effect that "you Orthodox Jews want to turn the clock back, you are against progress."

This evening, therefore, I want to invite you to accompany me in an analysis of the idea of progress from a broader and more informed point of view. Let us see if we all always mean what we say when we talk of "progress;" let us stop playing with slogans and analyze concepts; let us see if it is not true that sometimes you get the right time when you "turn the clock back," whether Orthodoxy is really doing that, and whether sometimes you must take a step backwards in the right direction.

I think it was Abe Lincoln who, over one hundred years ago, pointed to one of the commonest fallacies of our age, one

* Feb 3, 1956

which is most tragic in its consequences, when he said that "too many people mistake change for progress." No, change by itself is absolutely meaningless; you can change for the worse as well as for the good.

Of course, it would be most silly for us to say that we should give up the real advances of civilization. Modern man has made some terrific, good progress. The Salk vaccine, the unfolding of democratic government and the strides made in psychiatry, to mention only a few of the numerous advances we have made, are here to stay, we hope, and will always be a monument to the great constructive and creative forces unleashed by modern civilization. But as even the most radical modernist will admit, our moral and ethical progress has been left behind in the race to keep up with technology. We have not more but perhaps less great moral insights than the generations – or some generations – of the past had. Theoretical physics has given us radiological treatment of cancer, but also the hydrogen bomb; gynecology has given us greater protection for human beings, but also barbarians who boast of the ability to sterilize a hundred Jewesses a day – and are let off scot-free. Philosophy has produced many giants and many masterpieces, but not one has been able to approach the Torah, the Ten Commandments.

Indeed, since the giving of the Ten Commandments we have a startling number of developments in human thought. Instead of "I am the Lord your God," we have been told that Science or Man, or Psychology is our god. Instead of destroying idols, we have regenerated them in new forms. Instead of murder, Neitzche blazed the path for making a virtue of it, and Hitler applied the philosophy. Don't steal? Marx had a different philosophy, and Lenin and Stalin applied it in Communism. No adultery? Kinsey has documented the antiquity and irrelevancy of that mitzva. Indeed, the world has changed. But who will maintain that it is not time to take a step backwards in the right direction? If returning to that day on Sinai 3,500 years ago is "turning the clock back," I am all for it.

Going even further back in the annals of mankind, we again discover that the greatest progress was composed not always of change, but equally as much by rediscovering lost insights of the dim past. Most modern anthropologists have assumed that in the dawn of mankind humans were superstitious idol-worshippers, and only after many centuries was there developed the belief of One God. More recently, however, a good number of prominent scholars have changed their minds. Scientists like Andrew Lang and Engell now maintain that in its dawn, humanity had a monotheistic belief, and only afterwards did it degenerate into polytheism, idolatry and the like, until the fathers of the Jewish people recaptured the lost insights and proclaimed, "*Shema Yisrael Hashem Elokeinu Hashem Eḥad*, Hear, O Israel: Hashem is our God, Hashem, the One and Only" (Deuteronomy 6:4). Thus, we know that Paleolithic man (of the Stone Age) had a magical cult for his religion, i.e. he was a pagan who fashioned his idols out of stone. But, many anthropologists now say, pre-Paleolithic man believed in one author of all existence! (See G.W. Anderson, *Hebrew Religion*.)

But are the anthropologists the first to discover this fact, the fact that religion has frequently retrogressed instead of progressed with time? Decidedly not! Basing himself on obvious biblical texts in Genesis, and confirming material in the Talmud and Midrash, Maimonides (*Hilkhot Avoda Zara*, chapter 1) shows how originally man's faith was pure and noble, and that later idolatry appeared and corrupted this pure faith.

What do we see from all this? We see that Abraham, who propounded the belief in one God, took a step backwards in the right direction, even as ten generations before him, Noah did the same thing. We see that Moses, in transmitting the Ten Commandments, took a step backwards in the right direction. Of course, so much of what Moses gave – God's Torah – was new and bold. But in essence, it was a return to a purer and higher and nobler conception of life. That is what our Rabbis meant when they said that Abraham and the other Patriarchs observed the whole of the Torah! When a man is walking straight to the brink of a precipice where he can fall to his death, then taking a step backwards means going in the right direction. And that is true morally and religiously as well.

So that Orthodoxy, if at times it insists upon a return to old concepts and ideas, is certainly going in the right direction, not in the wrong direction. But is it "making progress?" I have been saving that term for clearer definition. That word has become a political slogan, preempted by anyone who wants to sell his idea to unthinking people. We automatically assume that the word progress is a synonym for good and decent and holy. So much so is this idea ingrained in the modern mind that I hesitated to include this discussion in my sermon. Someone might leave this synagogue and tell his neighbor, "Rabbi Lamm is solidly against progress. He said so himself." I beg of you, therefore, even if I should tell you that I am against certain kinds of "progress," keep it a secret. A rabbi should never be, I am told, on the unpopular side.

Allow me to read to you, in this connection, a short passage by the late Ludwig Lewisohn which I read in his short masterpiece, *The American Jew*. Speaking of the fact that so many Jews have come back to a realization of the eternal values of Judaism, he says:

> More and more Jews are confronting this inner act of recognition and re-alliance within themselves. But when they seek to draw the right inferences in action, when they set out to change their lives, they are met, from many quarters... with the cry: "But you cannot do that in this world and age; do you think the clock can be set back? We are in the middle of the twentieth century. History races on." Ah yes, history races on; every age has been progressive. The Latin word from which "progressive" comes, the verb "progredior," means to march forward. Forward – to what goal? A murderer marches forward to the scene of his crime.

Forward movement in space or time has no virtue of its own. The quality of the goal of movement determines the quality of the act. People are foolishly proud of being, as the silly saying goes, "forward-looking." To what do they look forward? Usually to a multiplication of the sins and evils with which man is already afflicted.

Well, there you have it. And few could express it better than the man who has been called the greatest stylist in the English language of the twentieth century. The slogan "progress" or "forward-looking" has no virtue of its own. And quote Lewisohn, not me, if you tell this to someone else.

You have asked me, just last week, in full and genuine sincerity, if the invention of the incandescent electric bulb has not outmoded the laws of Shabbat and the principle of recognition of God's creation and Lordship of the Universe. And this week I ask you, in the same sincerity, if the invention of the hydrogen bomb and cobalt bomb has not created a new need for just such laws and just such recognition. The mere invention of new tools does not make religion outdated, any more than the invention of new stone idols by Paleolithic man made the earlier belief in one God out of date, and superstition right.

Human nature has not changed much these last thousands of years. Man is still gripped by love and by hate, by sympathy and meanness, by superstition and by insight, by a passion for justice and by just plain passion. The teachings expounded on Sinai 3,500 years ago, teaching man to repress the hate, the meanness, the superstition and the passion and lust and bring out the love and sympathy and insight and compassion, they are central to the solution of man's moral crisis no matter when he lives; they are completely independent of the tools he has forged and the extent of his mathematical knowledge. Murder remains murder whether committed by a Paleolithic man or by a modern scientist. And idolatry is perhaps more sinful when committed by contemporary man than when resorted to by a primitive.

Rereading the portion of the week and the Ten Commandments our ancestors heard at Sinai as the earth quaked and the heavens exploded, we too must be gripped by a new strength and a new courage and a new insight. We must learn to resist the onslaught of empty slogans and hollow epithets. We must learn to seek for that which is good, whether that lies in the past or in the future. We must learn that God does not change, but that man must; and that that change must be in the direction of God. We must learn to understand that frequently we are called upon to take a step backwards in the right direction.

Thirteen
In the Days of Smallness*

THERE IS AN IMPRESSION CURRENT IN OUR SOCIETY that religion is solely a question of emotion. If you feel inspired, in the mood, then you believe, you worship, you observe. But if you are not subjectively attuned to religion, if you do not feel a powerful need for it, if you are not grasped by it, then it is meaningless and irrelevant for you. Some people go so far as to say that he who does not experience deep emotions and does not feel great stirrings, yet prays and observes religious duties, is a hypocrite.

Religion, according to this interpretation, is a subjective experience, a reaction of an autonomous personality, reflecting the moods and needs of man. If you have a feeling for it, then religion is for you; otherwise, keep away from it. Can traditional Judaism agree with this romanticized notion of religion, so popular today?

To an extent, there are several romantic elements present in classical Judaism, and they are highlighted especially by the movement known as Hasidism. Thus, Judaism knows of, and Hasidism emphasizes, the inwardness of *kavana*, the inspiration of *deveikut*, the joy of *simḥa shel mitzva*, the outpouring of genuine emotions and ecstasy. It is these that distinguish

* January 27, 1962

Hasidism as a unique movement in Judaism. The subjective, human experience of religion is present in all of Judaism but lies at the very heart of Hasidism.

But does this mean that without the emotional outpouring, without the feeling of inspiration, that there is nothing left? That Torah no longer can place any demands upon a man?

Of course not. We must never confuse Hasidism, which is an authentic religious movement, with this pale and shallow sentimentalism of our age. For the modern temper recognizes religion as "man-made," as issuing from the recesses of the human psyche alone. But Judaism firmly maintains that Torah comes from God, that it has clear claims upon the human being, that it is objectively valid, independent of human sentiments. Hasidism too recognizes these eternally valid divine claims; only it taught that it is better to react to God and respond to His demand with joy, with feeling, with ecstasy. But the total claim of Torah certainly goes beyond the passing moods of temperamental humans.

This problem is a real one for moderns. We live in a mundane, secularized world, in a highly technological society in which it is not easy to find inspiration. Our culture encourages bashfulness, not the natural overflow of emotions; experiments, not experiences; facts, not feelings. We do not normally feel the urge to pray in utter devotion, to learn Torah for the sake of Heaven, to observe mitzvot because we love God. If we accept this popular thesis that all religion is a matter of human moods, then, for all practical purposes, Torah must vanish from the world. Those who wait for "inspiration" to pray usually do not pray.

It is this problem to which the Baal Shem Tov, the sainted founder of the Hasidic movement, addressed himself in a comment on this morning's *parasha*. In the description of the revelation of Torah at Sinai we read, "And they stood at the bottom of the mountain" (Exodus 19:17).

Our Rabbis of the Talmud (*Shabbat 88a*) commented as follows: "The Lord lifted up Mount Sinai like a barrel above their heads and said: if you accept the Torah, good and well; if not, I shall lower the mountain on your head, and here shall be your collective graves." God "chose" the people of Israel; they literally had no choice.

What do we, as individuals, learn from this? The Baal Shem Tov, quoted by his famous disciple Rabbi Yaakov Yosef, states the following: "This teaches us that even when a man does not have an overwhelming desire for Torah or the service of the Lord, nevertheless, he is not free to desist from them; he must imagine as if someone is forcing him to perform these duties against his will, just as God coerced the children of Israel into accepting the Torah at Sinai." And the Baal Shem Tov concludes, "and this is the good way for a Jewish man to follow during the *yemei hakatnut*, the days of smallness" (*Tzofnat Pane'aḥ, Parashat Shemot*).

There are days – nay, years and decades – when we are small; our capacities sorely limited, our spirit puny, our soul desiccated, our sensitivity parched, our hearts shrunken and dried up. Society pushes us towards a constant trivialization. We are immersed in petty details, lost in the shallowness of little problems, little people, and a little self. We abjure large visions, we deny depth, we ignore our own large capacity for experiencing lofty emotions, for an awareness of the transcendent, for a sense of the mysterious, for the daring to lift the veil of everyday life and catch a glimpse of the grandeur and majesty that lie just beyond the world of money and machines, shipping and shopping.

And in these *yemei hakatnut*, when we cannot summon up the spirit from the resources within us, in these days too, we must not desist from prayer, from Torah, from mitzvot. Just as *klal Yisrael* accepted the Torah because God chose them and coerced them into it, so we as individuals, in the "days of smallness," must force ourselves to do and observe, to live and obey, according to the word of God, *as if* we were big, inspired, uplifted.

There is no greater *pleasure*, says Baal Shem Tov, than *davening* or studying Torah during the *yemei hagadlut*, when we feel fully inspired, alert to the whisper of divinity all about us. But there is no greater *reward*, he continues, for practicing the discipline of one's self that results in observing, in studying, in practicing Jewishness during the *yemei hakatnut*! For the only way to arrive at *gadlut*, greatness, is to live responsibly and respectfully through the periods of *katnut*, smallness. Those who are defeated by triviality and pettiness cannot hope to succeed to greatness and eminence. Only he who can *daven Minḥa* in his office, despite a crowded calendar and a mind cluttered with commonplaces, can hope, someday, to experience true *gadlut*, an exquisite *aliyat neshama* – the soaring of the soul and ascension of the spirit – during a *Neila* service or another very special occasion. Only a person who studies Torah and attends classes regularly despite an inner inertia will someday experience the unique, full, and breathless joy in perceiving new intellectual horizons and spiritual vistas in Torah itself. For Torah is not primarily a matter of human moods; it is primarily a matter of the divine will. If we respond to that will when we are caught up in the moods of mediocrity, in *yemei hakatnut*, then it will be His will to grant us loftier, more sublime, and more exalted experiences of *gadlut*.

The man who prays only when he is moved to do so, who studies only when he is overwhelmed by intellectual curiosity is like a mother who feeds her child only when she is inspired by his loveliness rather when the child is hungry, or like the husband who is faithful to his wife only when he feels stirred by a great love for her. It is a sure recipe for remaining forever stranded in the stagnating swamps of smallness; the *yemei hakatnut*.

Hasidim tell the following story: There was a small hamlet to which travelers from the outside world came only very rarely. One day, the townspeople noticed that their watches were not synchronized. Every watch showed a different time, so that most likely no one had the right time. As a result, all the townspeople except one put their watches on their shelves and failed to wind them. This one man said: although I am sure I do not have the right time, nevertheless, I will keep my watch wound. Several months later, a traveler chanced upon the hamlet. The people surrounded him and asked him for news from the outside world, and then for the right time. He took out his watch and told them. The people ran back to recover their watches and set them properly. But, lo and behold, none of the watches would work, for they had grown rusty, except the watch which this one man had kept winding all along despite the ridicule of his friends.

So it is with prayer, or Torah, or any other religious duty. Unless you keep it "running" constantly it will be of no avail to you in the moments of crisis when you really need it. He who cannot abide them during the "days of smallness," when he knows that his soul is not synchronized with sublimity, that man will fail during the opportunities of the "days of greatness." He will be rusty. His prayer will be puny, his worship an abortion, his study of Torah a frustration.

The Kotzker Rebbe asked: why, in the *Shema* (Deuteronomy 6:4), do we read, "and these words shall be on your heart?" Why do we say, "*al levavekha*, on your heart" and why not, "*bilevavekha*, in your heart?" And the Kotzker Rebbe answers: it is not too often that the heart is open and that the words of God can enter directly into it. Usually the heart is closed, indifferent, and even callous. Yet the Torah demands that if the words of the Lord cannot come right into an open heart, then at least they shall be placed on the closed heart, so that during those moments of greatness and inspiration, when the human heart suddenly opens up, then the words of Torah which had been piled on it will tumble in and fill the heart with the seeds of true greatness and sublimity. The reward for the strenuous efforts made during the long, dreary, dismal, and uninspired *yemei hakatnut* comes during these rare but precious moments of *gadlut*.

"May the words of my mouth be pleasing to You, and the meditation of my heart come before You, O Lord my Rock and Redeemer" (*Shemoneh Esrei*). Even when, during the "days of smallness," only my lips move and only my mouth speak, but my heart remains mute and my spirit sunk in a stony silence, even then may my efforts be pleasing to You. So that, when, during the "days of greatness," my heart opens up, then may the meditations of my heart rise up before You in all their pristine glory. For You, O Lord, are *tzuri*, my Rock, who supports me in my weakness and smallness; and also *go'ali*, my Redeemer, who raises me on high and gives wings to my soul during my moments of greatness.

Celebrating Shavuot

Fourteen
This Very Day*

WE MUST BE HONEST AND ADMIT THAT THE STUDY OF Torah, of which we speak this festival of Shavuot, is in serious trouble. Every rabbi knows that the best way to anesthetize his congregation is to speak to them about the duty of *talmud Torah*. There is hardly a more effective method of putting people to sleep.

Why is that so? Why the widespread disrepute of that commandment about which it is said, "*talmud Torah keneged kulam*, the study of Torah is superior to all others?"

It is not because our congregations are unintelligent. By and large, they are as intelligent as any congregations of the past, and a good deal more cultured.

It is not because they do not have sufficient Jewish education. The refusal even to give the proposal of adult *talmud Torah* a fair hearing is as characteristic of those who have studied Jewish sources as those who have not.

The reason for this sorry state of affairs is, I believe, that the study of Torah is so very impractical. People ask: what does it lead to? What diploma do you get as a result? When is the end in sight? Can it get me a better job? Will it help feed the poor or save refugees?

---

* June 3, 1968

We are so distressed by its apparent impracticality that even we Orthodox Jews, when we occasionally hear about a young man who has devoted his life solely to the study of Torah, react with annoyance. What will he accomplish with it? Whom does he help? Let him get a job and make a living!

We cannot abide impractical occupations. We are a vocation and work-oriented society. Secular man is, above all, a pragmatist. Ideas must work, principles must have application, theories must forthwith produce results. When two modern, secular men discuss a third person, they do not ask, "Who is he," or, "What kind of person is he," but, "What does he do?" What a man *does* – what he accomplishes, what he achieves, the results he produces – that is what defines his very self. In a civilization of this sort we have lost the capacity for appreciating anything for its own sake; we look only for that which is beyond it, that to which it leads.

Today, therefore, I do not want to preach to you *that* we ought to study Torah, but to recommend *how* we might go about it. Perhaps some of these hints as to method and technique will induce us to do that which is our chief obligation as Jews.

First, we must turn the tables on ourselves. Instead of asking of what use the study of Torah is, we must ask whether routine work in business and profession really makes sense, whether they are, ultimately, as meaningful and useful and practical as we tell ourselves.

This holiday of Shavuot, our *zeman matan Toratenu*, the time of the giving of the Torah, is a summons to us to pause in the midst of all our frenzied activities for a moment of reflection: we consider our daily work and occupations eminently practical, because they lead to something else. Then we must ask ourselves, concerning our business or professions, the same question we ask of the study of Torah: Why? For what purpose? What do we want to make all this money for? What, after all, does all this lead to?

That is a painful question. We usually seek to avoid such ultimate challenges.

Well, what for? Usually the answer is for our children. But I do not think that answer sufficient.

It is told of the Ḥozeh (Seer) of Lublin that he once accosted one of his people who was rushing in the marketplace. "Come with me to the study hall so that we may study Torah," the rabbi said to the harried man. "No, Rabbi," he answered, "I can't because I am in a hurry." The rabbi pressed, "But why not, why can't you come with me now?" Again came the response, "I have to make a living." "But," the rabbi continued, "What for? What do you need the money for?" The man answered, quite naturally and logically, "I've got to make money for my children." The rabbi appeared satisfied.

Some twenty years later, the rabbi, who was apparently a persistent personality, accosted another man on the street and the same dialogue ensued. Finally, the rabbi looked deeply into the man's eyes and said to him, "Why, I recognize you! I had the same encounter and the same conversation with your father just twenty years ago. At that time, he also told me that he was too busy to study Torah because he had to make a living for his children. And now you tell me that you must make a living for *your* children. When, O God Almighty, will I meet that one human being for whom all the generations labored so mightily?"

We are caught in a vicious cycle. We allow our religious talents to atrophy because we must make money for our children, but they too do not have the time for leisure, for developing their spiritual dimensions. They must work to make money for *their* children, and their children for their children...

We delude ourselves if we think that our profane activities make much more practical sense than our supposedly unworldly pursuit of Torah. We fool ourselves if we think that our business occupations have any more lasting value than *talmud Torah* for its own sake. Usually we only permit ourselves to become befuddled by our busy-ness. Most of the time we are engaged in motion, not movement; in activity, not action. Perhaps this realization of the ultimate impracticality of our profane labors will dull the sharp edge of our presumptuous challenge to *talmud Torah*. Maybe, after all, things don't have to be quite so pragmatically useful.

Second, in addition to questioning whether our reputedly practical labors are really so worthwhile, we must have a clear understanding of the importance of the study of Torah in the Jewish tradition. Nachmanides makes an interesting observation concerning one of the verses in the Torah about the festival of Shavuot. We read, "*Ukeratem be'etzem hayom hazeh mikra kodesh*, and you shall call on this very day a holy convocation" (Leviticus 23:21). Nachmanides is intrigued by the phrase "*be'etzem hayom hazeh*, on this very day." There is only one other place in the Torah where this appears, and that is with regard to Yom Kippur: "*vekhol melakha lo taasu be'etzem hayom hazeh*, and you shall do no form of work on this very day" (Leviticus 23:28).

What is the affinity between Shavuot and Yom Kippur, such that both of them are referred to as applying to *be'etzem hayom hazeh*, this very day?

I suggest that just as Yom Kippur is not considered primarily the recollection of an historical event, but its importance is for its own sake, for the atonement that it gives on its own account, so the study of Torah is not just a ceremony or a ritual or a commemoration of something else, but is in and of itself sacred.

Furthermore, it means that just as Yom Kippur is effective in offering atonement only if one fasts on *etzem hayom hazeh*, on this very day of Yom Kippur, so the study of Torah must be done on *etzem hayom hazeh*, this very day – every single day! No matter what day it is, on *etzem hayom hazeh* one must study Torah; it brooks no postponement. Torah is not an activity which I undertake for the sake of doing any other activities;

the reverse is true: this activity of Torah is the purpose of all else, whether sacred or profane.

The Talmud presents to us a remarkable idea (*Berakhot* 35b). Rabbi Yishmael makes the following comment: we know that Torah must be studied constantly. "And you shall meditate in it by day and by night" (Joshua 1:8). But if that is the case, and if we are to take the Bible with all seriousness, then man must study all the time, whether by day or by night, and have no time to pursue any other interests or activities, even to pursue working to support himself and his family. How, then do we know that man is indeed permitted to work for a living? He answers: we read in the second passage of the *Shema* the verse "and you shall gather in your corn and your wine and your oil" (Deuteronomy 11:14). Thus, the Bible explicitly tells us that we are permitted to work at profane activities, to gather in our harvest, to make a living. From this we know, concludes Rabbi Yishmael, that a man is permitted to spend time away from Torah in order to advance his livelihood. What this means, therefore, is that Torah is the main activity of life, and we may do other things only because they enhance this major activity of our existence. It is not that we must study a little Torah during our lifetime which is devoted primarily to business or profession, but that the time we spend in our secular activities is only a *heter*, a special dispensation, for time taken away from our only legitimate activity, namely, *talmud Torah*.

This awareness of the special nature of Torah study leads us to a further point: successful pursuit of Torah study is a matter of timing. The Rabbis tell us that after a man dies and he comes before the Heavenly Court, he is asked, amongst other things: *Kavata itim leTorah* – Did you set aside time for the study of Torah? (*Shabbat* 31a). The first word of that question derives from the root K-V-A, which in Rabbinic language means to set a regular time aside. We must, therefore, not study haphazardly but regularly.

Yet a distinguished Hasidic teacher, who was also one of the foremost Talmudic authorities of his age, Rav Pinchas Horowitz (disciple of the Maggid MiMizritch), adds an unusual insight (*Sefer Hafla'a*, introduction to *Ketubot* 36). It is true, he says, that a man must put aside regular time for his study. But in addition, the sweetest study of Torah occurs during the times that are unscheduled! That very root, K-V-A, in biblical Hebrew means something quite different from "to set aside." It means "to steal" (*Rosh Hashana* 26b). A man, he tells us, must *steal* time for Torah! Thus, the prophet Malachi says, "*hayikba adam Elokim* – Can a man *steal* from God?" (Malachi 3:8). Not only must man schedule time for Torah, but he must take time away from other scheduled activities in order to add these cherished moments to the study of Torah. I personally find that most creative work is done in those precious little patches of time snatched here and there, from other, duller activities.

If indeed we have the right conception of the value of Torah in Judaism, namely, that like Yom Kippur, Torah is an autonomous value which must be pursued this very day, that it is the real stuff of life from which we may only occasionally be excused, then we shall certainly be willing to steal time for all else in order to indulge in *talmud Torah*.

Finally, and this is especially relevant to the day that we recite *Yizkor*, the effective pursuit of the study of Torah in our own days requires a reflective attitude towards life as such.

Permit me to relate to you a charming story which, like its author, sounds naive and unsophisticated and simple, yet underneath it all reveals a brooding wisdom that is truly profound. And if this tale touches some raw psychological nerve by a tinge of morbidity, it may be worth it in the results that it produces.

The great Chofetz Chaim commented on the Rabbinic statement that "Torah can exist and flourish only for one who is willing to kill himself for it" (*Berakhot* 63b). Once, he relates, there was a poor Jewish couple in Lithuania who opened a grocery store in a village which was entirely non-Jewish. They worked hard and labored long hours. Every morning the husband would make his way to the nearby town so that he could pray his morning services with the *minyan* – which real Jew does not make an effort to pray with a *minyan*? – and return as soon as possible. He would come late, and return early, in order that his wife would not have to be alone in the store for too long a time. But as time went on, the store appealed to him less and the synagogue appealed to him more. He came at the beginning of the services and left at the end. Gradually the time increased: he came earlier for the reading of some Psalms and left later after the lesson in Talmud. Towards the High Holiday season, he had to come even earlier in order to be present for the *Seliḥot* service. His wife was distraught, discovering that she was spending a great part of the day by herself in the store, and she complained about it.

That evening the husband came home and said to her, "My dear, I have something very important to discuss with you."

"Is anything wrong?" she asked, disturbed.

"Do not worry, my dear," he continued, "but I do want to talk to you about something important. You know, that sooner or later we are going to die." He noticed that his wife was even more distressed, expecting the worst, but he continued: "No, there is nothing wrong, but I would like you to listen further. You know that I am several years older than you, and I probably shall go first. Now tell me, my dear, what will you do after I am gone? How will you support yourself?" Whereupon, the poor wife dissolved in tears at the mere contemplation of her husband's mortality and her own eventual widowhood. After a while, however, she replied: "I suppose the only way to survive will be my continuing the store and making whatever I can."

"In other words," her husband said, "you would be able to manage the store by yourself, even if I am not around?"

"Yes," the wife said, "if I have no choice, I will have to and I will succeed."

"In that case, dear wife," said the husband, "I must ask you for a favor. I hope that the two of us will live to 120 years, but, as long as I live, I ask you to imagine that every morning I have died for half an hour... Just assume that for a short part of each day you are on your own, even as eventually you will probably have to be..."

Indeed, Torah can flourish and thrive only when a man is willing to die for it, i.e., when he is willing to take time out of a busy schedule and to be "dead to the world" in order to be alive to his own spiritual personality, alive to his God, alive to the whole heritage of Judaism. To die a little bit to the harried superficialities of everyday life, is to let yourself live more deeply and much longer for the things that really count. One of the ways of doing this is to destroy, psychologically, that myth of our indispensability. We will find more time for the study of Torah, more time for the synagogue, more time for our families, if we recognize that we are not really indispensable to the functioning of our business, to the survival of society, to the progress of our professions.

Let us imagine that we are temporarily departed, that we vanish for a little part of the day from our earthly scene, and devote that extra time to studying Torah, to attending to our spiritual welfare, to spending a bit more time with wife and children. It is a greater measure of wisdom to imagine that we were dead so that we might live all the better. In that way, we may make less of a living, but we will live more life.

On this festival of the giving of the Torah, we must think deeply of our own responsibility to study that Torah, and not only to send our children to learn it. We must call an end to this American propensity for relegating Torah to the extremes of early childhood and post-retirement leisure years, to make of Torah an exercise of either pediatrics or geriatrics, and to leave the major part of life in between as a gaping vacuum.

As we ponder the means we have mentioned to make Talmud Torah more meaningful and increase our desire to study it, let us bear in mind its lofty rewards. If the way to Torah is to recognize that it makes demands on us *be'etzem hayom hazeh*, this very day every day, then remember that it also grants us more than this one very day; it bestows upon us all of eternity, even as we say when we are about to study the Torah that "*vehayei olam nata betokheinu*, it implants in us eternal life."

If the way to get at the study of Torah is by stealing time and by pondering our own absence from this worldly scene, then let us remember that its reward is wealth for our act of noble stealing, and length of days for our temporary demises. "*Orekh yamim biyemina, bismola osher vekhavod*, length of days is at the right hand of Torah, and in its left hand is wealth and honor" (*Proverbs* 3:16).

Fifteen
Shavuot Derives from Shevua*

THE NAME OF THIS HOLIDAY, SHAVUOT, WHICH CELEbrates the giving of Torah at Mount Sinai is usually explained as deriving from the word *shavua*, meaning weeks, because it comes at the end of seven weeks counted from the second day of Passover. There is another explanation, however, offered by the Gerer Rebbe in his *S'fat Emet* which sheds a new light on the entire festival and the nature of the relation of each and every one of us to Torah itself. He maintains that the word *shavuot* comes from the word *shevua*, meaning an oath or a vow. This he derives from the Talmudic statement that every Jew is *mushba ve'omed mehar sinai,* in a state of oath consummated at Mount Sinai (*Yoma* 73b) to observe the Torah and all its commandments. Shavuot, therefore, is the time that each of us reaffirms the essence of our relationship with Torah – not an easy-going friendship, not just pride in it, not the use of it for private ends – but *shevua*, an oath, a sacred and inviolable vow.

Those of us who keep abreast of current religious writings will recognize that idea in one word used very frequently,

---

* May 16, 1956

"commitment." To be religious means to be committed to Torah, to submit to it without reservation or qualification. The Bible calls it *berit* or covenant, the Talmud calls it *shevua* or vow, Hasidism calls it *devekut* or attachment, modern thinkers call it "commitment" or "the leap of faith." But call it what you will, it means the same thing: the knowledge that the whole essence of your life is intertwined with Torah, that you live only by the Law of God, that otherwise life has no meaning for you. It means you are bound to Torah, and stray from it though you may, it is all you have, all your life, and that you recognize this and only this as truth.

In a modified way all of you will recognize what we mean by this *shevua*, this idea of vow or commitment. When, as children, some of us may have belonged to the Boy Scouts, we committed ourselves to the principles of good citizenship, kindness and so on. Marriage is a kind of commitment – a pledge to live up to certain standards of monogamous behavior, to considerate treatment of one's spouse, to domestic happiness and peacefulness. When as businessmen you sign a contract – that is a commitment; you commit yourself to buy or sell or otherwise deal in a certain specific manner. Once you signed you simply cannot withdraw, for you have made a commitment. Those of us who were born abroad and were naturalized as citizens, submitted to a commitment – to protect our country and remain ever loyal to it. Unless commitment has value, all of life becomes an unmapped and treacherous jungle. Commitment is, in reality, the essence of civilization.

But what we reaffirm on this holiday of Shavuot, the vow or commitment to Torah, is even more drastic than all that. The concept of *shevua*, of commitment to Torah, is more than risking membership in a club or business reputation or citizenship or married life. It means that you stake your very life on your commitment. It involves the totality of all your existence, it is either all or nothing insofar as the meaning of life and the validity of any principles you may have.

Perhaps that is one of the reasons we read the Book of Ruth today. Its most moving passage, the decision of Ruth to remain with her destitute mother-in-law Naomi, is the best description ever given of real, total commitment. Recall those stirring words, spoken by this young widow to her old and also widowed mother-in-law: "...wherever you go, I will go, and where you lodge, I will lodge; your people shall be my people, and your God, my God; where you die, I will die, and there will I be buried; the Lord do to me, and more also, if anything but death parts you and me" (Ruth 1:16). There are no ifs and buts in this proposition. It is commitment pure and simple. It is *shevua*, even as the language indicates, "thus may the Lord do to me." Ruth, the stranger, the lonely young widow, swore and knew what she was swearing to. It was a commitment not only to Naomi, but to her people and her God; it was the sacred vow that our people gave at Sinai, that makes each of us a *mushba ve'omed mehar sinai*, but which she, being a non-Jew, now undertook on her own for the first time. "*VeRut davka ba*" (Ruth 1:14). There was *devekut*, attachment, vow, covenant, commitment, leap of faith. No wonder we read this Book on Shavuot! It tells us in no uncertain terms how we are to relate ourselves to our inheritance – a reaffirmation of total, uncompromising vow.

So that saying *amen* to the *shevua* taken by our people at the foot of Sinai, reaffirming that sacred vow and total commitment, means that you have committed your whole life – your needs and desires, your dreams and ambitions, your acts and your thoughts, all these must now find expression in and through Torah.

When you realize the consequences of that *shevua*, you begin to understand that it took a lot of courage and that to do so today takes just as much courage. Committing ourselves to Torah means that we are going to restrain ourselves and deny ourselves certain things because of it. For the adolescents here this morning that commitment meant giving up precious school work for these two days. For the adults, two important business days. For all of us it means curbing our appetites and desires. Indeed, we stake our lives on that vow.

At this point, someone here may be inclined to think: well, if it's that inclusive, can't I just go along without a real commitment? If a *shevua* to Torah involves a whole new way of practical life and a positive belief in God and Torah and prophecy and the redemption of Israel – can't I have the privilege of suspending my judgement? Can't I remain neutral and not sign my life on the dotted line? Must I say "yes" or "no"? After all, I have my doubts concerning many of these things, must I make my mind up once and for all?

The name for that attitude of neutrality is called agnosticism – suspended judgement, neither belief nor disbelief. It is perhaps the most fashionable of all attitudes. It gives the agnostic the comfortable feeling of being a detached, scientific observer, above allegiance and commitment. And our answer to that is: it's impossible. You may be able to avoid forming an opinion. But you can't avoid doing something with your life. At Sinai, the Talmud (*Shabbat* 88a) tells us, God raised the mountain over the assembled Israelites and told them, "if you accept the Torah, good; if not, I will drop this mountain on you, and here shall be your grave!" Even our Rabbis were shocked by this statement, and one even said "in that case we're not responsible, we were forced to accept" (Rashi, *Shabbat* 88a).

I suggest, however, a different interpretation of that great and crucial event. God did not force us to accept. He did force us to choose. It is not that we had no choice; it is that we had no choice but to choose. You see, God told Israel, and us, life has its forced decisions. There are certain things about which you have got to decide whether you like it or not. And if you don't choose of your own free will, "here shall be your grave!" – then that is death itself, for life chooses for you. There is no such thing as neutrality in the great issues. It is one way or the other. It is a fact of momentous significance: you can escape making up your mind, but you cannot escape living your life as if you had made it up one way or the other. You can avoid deciding if the moon has livable atmosphere or vegetation. But you can't avoid making up your life on the question of Torah. Either this world is aimless and life is without purpose, in which case you will live it as freely and wildly as you can with only one interest – your selfish indulgence – or it has a goal and a purpose, there is a God, He gave a Torah, we were created in His image – in which case we will live our lives according to His Torah, fulfill the purpose for which we came into being and enhance that divine image. Intellectually you may quibble about it. But insofar as life – real life actual living – is concerned, either you live as if there were a God or as if there were no God. "Neutrality" is only a figment of an unhealthy imagination. In this case it really is a choice – that there is no God, a commitment to the proposition that life is an accident, purposeless, meaningless, a blind alley in an uncertain evolution. What we are here for on this Shavuot day is to affirm that there is either commitment for or against, one way or the other, and that we cast our lot with Torah – that is the *kabalat haTorah*, the *shevua* that we are here to make.

The halakha indicated that idea when it said, in the words of Maimonides (*Hilkhot Shevuot* 2,12): that *shevua* or commitment means something, only when the heart intends all that the mouth says. To talk about "Jewish consciousness" or "Jewish survival," to urge others to be "proud" of their "heritage," without living a thoroughly Jewish existence yourself, that shows a discrepancy between heart and mouth, it proves that there is a feeling of so-called neutrality on the basic question, it points to no commitment at all. Real commitment to Torah, real *shevua*, demands the totality of one's life. It is more than a word of honor. It is a life of honor.

One more extremely important fact should be mentioned about the nature of this commitment to Torah. And that is, it is not only a pledge that requires the courage to give, to yield, to relinquish and sacrifice. There is another facet to it: the courage to receive, to benefit, to hope. In the Torah, *shevuat bitui* is both *lehara o lehetiv* (Leviticus 5:4), to vow whether to do good or bad. The halakha interprets that as: to do or not to do, positive or negative oaths, to give or to receive. That is true as well of the commitment to Torah, the *shevua* at Mount Sinai which we relive today.

Commitment to Torah means not only the self-control not to smoke on Shabbat, but the strength, as well, to put all disturbing thoughts out of my mind and allow it to be exposed to the sacred and pleasant serenity of Shabbos.

Shevua means *bitaḥon* – to dare to hope, to know that even when *"avi ve'imi azavuni*, when parents and friends have forsaken me, *Hashem yaasfeni*, that God befriends me" (Psalms 27:10).

Commitment means to stake my life on the confidence that even in the valley of the shadow of death, I will fear no evil, *"ki ata imadi*, for You are with me" (Psalms 23:4).

Shevua challenges me to the faith that even when Israel is surrounded by fierce enemies and betrayed by her friends, she will not go under, for, in the words of the *Akdamut*, "perfect joy and pure delight will come to Jerusalem when He will gather therein her exiles."

Commitment means that when doctors have despaired and relatives have given up, I will not abandon hope, for *"ani Hashem rofe'ekha"* (Exodus 15:26) – God is He who heals.

Shevua to Torah means the courage to know with all my heart and soul, despite the hard cynicism and pitiable confusion which surrounds me from all sides, that I must dare to believe that even death is not final, for "God who kills and brings down to the grave, brings up again and resurrects" (I Samuel 2:6).

This festival of Shavuot, then, is the time that we are called upon to reaffirm our *shevua* to God and His Torah, to declare that we are committed, that we cannot be neutral, that our hearts join our lips in expressing this loyalty and pledging this fealty, that our commitment is not only an obligation, but a privilege, not only to sacrifice but to serenity, not only to duty but to hope. We are in a state of oath from Sinai. The vows then made and the affirmations now pronounced bridge the gap of centuries, and announce to all the world and for all eternity that *Kudsha Berikh Hu, Yisrael, ve'Oraita ḥad hu* (*Zohar* 3:73), that God, Torah and Israel are solemnly pledged to each other in a sacred commitment that will not cease as long as day follows night and as long as the heavens are stretched above this earth.

Sixteen
Waiting*

THERE IS ONE PECULIAR ASPECT OF SHAVUOT WHICH marks it as different from other holidays. That is, is introduced by a three-day waiting period known as *Sheloshet Yemei Hagbala*. These three days are reserved for spiritual preparation for renewed commitment to the Torah, the revelation of which we commemorate on Shavuot, and they thus have the character of semi-festivals; hence, the *sefira* mourning regulations are suspended during these days.

The origin of this three-day waiting period goes back to the giving of the Torah itself at Mount Sinai. "And the Lord said to Moses: Go on to the people and sanctify them today and tomorrow... and be ready for the third day; for on the third day the Lord will come down upon Mount Sinai. And you shall set bounds unto the people roundabout, saying: take heed to yourselves, that you go not up to the mountain or touch the border of it; whosoever touches the mountain shall be surely put to death... When the ram's horns sound long, they shall come up to the mountain" (Exodus 19:10–13).

I say that this is "peculiar" and "different," and yet what it symbolizes is an extremely important and highly characteristic Jewish trait. And that is – waiting, the strength to bide one's time in the anticipation of some future event.

* May 19, 1972

For, indeed, waiting is a fundamental theme of all Jewish life. Judaism teaches the young man and woman to wait, sometimes a painful and heroic wait, from the time of physical maturation until the time of marriage, before expressing basic instinct. The New Morality sneers at us because of this. It tells young people that they are being inhibited by an obscurantist and dehumanizing Establishment code-morality. But such waiting is of the essence of Judaism.

For twenty centuries Jews have rejected alluring utopias and meretricious "saviors," and have continued waiting for the Messiah. Christianity condemns us for this. They tell us that the Messiah already came a long time ago. But we looked around the world, found it a rotten and corrupt as can be, and we decided that Messiah never came and that we are still waiting for him: "I believe in perfect faith in the coming of the Messiah, and though he tarry, nonetheless *I shall wait* for Him..."

Such waiting is not easy. It taxes one's patience, energy, and credibility. I have always liked the King James translation of the verse in Psalms "*kavei el Hashem*" (Psalms 27:14), which we would normally translate, "hope to the Lord." The classical English translation is, "wait upon the Lord." For wait means hope, but even more than that. It includes faith and confidence, strength and heroism, discipline and restraint. Indeed, the word *hagbalah* in *Sheloshet Yemei Hagbala*, implies restraint, the renunciation of easy victories. *Hagbala* symbolizes deferred gratification, the sign of both psychological and spiritual maturity. Clearly, all of Judaism is suffused with the principle of heroic waiting. And Eli Wiesel has discovered that waiting is one of the distinguishing characteristics of Hasidic tales.

So in our turbulent age, with shifting tastes and changing life-styles and brand new dogmas, where what was "in" yesterday is "way out" today, where old philosophies emerge and then decline from one issue of *Time* magazine to the next, where even religious thinkers suffer from what has been called "mood theologies," in a time of this sort we are befuddled and bewildered. Traditional, Orthodox Jews sometimes do not know what to think and what will come next. But Judaism gives us strength. It tells us, "Wait!" If you wait patiently, you will survive all these chimerical and ephemeral storms, and in the end truth will win out. Wait and survive – and triumph. The pre-Shavuot three-day waiting period is a reminder of the Jewish capacity to wait, the warning not to hurry even onto Mount Sinai and to receiving the Torah. The quickest way to lose one's head is by a headlong rush. For eagerness leads to impatience, and impatience to impetuousness, and that to rashness, and that usually ends up as recklessness.

Not only ordinary people are subject to the temptations of impatience. Even giants can fail. When Moses was atop Mount Sinai, God told him, "Go down, charge the people, lest they break through onto the Lord to gaze, and many of them will perish" (Exodus 19:21). The people will find it difficult to wait. They will be overwhelmed by anxiety and curiosity, and their impatience will get the better of them, "*venafal mimenu rav*, many of them will perish." But the Aramaic translator Targum Jonathan renders that last word *rav* somewhat differently: "and the greatest of them will fall." The word *rav* means not "many" in this instance, but, as Rashi mentions: *mufla*, the most distinguished, the *rav*. Waiting is a sore trial, even for the greatest of people!

And yet, that is only half the story. There is an equal and opposite danger of endless procrastination. It was Aristotle who taught us that vice is often virtue taken to excess (Book II of Aristotle's *Nicomachean Ethics*). Waiting too long is frequently a rationalization for acquiescence to evil, and a super-abundance of tolerance to injustice and wretchedness. Wait too long and all your sacrifices will be in vain.

Not waiting is a sign of impulsiveness and immaturity. But endless waiting is a symptom of moral arthritis and psychological atrophy and the creeping paralysis of the spirit. It is a form of disguised despair.

When the Jews were in Egypt, our tradition teaches us, they were redeemed at the very last instant possible, just as they sank into the 49th of the 50 degrees of impurity and spiritual corruption. Had the redemption or Exodus been delayed by one hour, it would have been too late, for the Israelites would have fallen to the very 50th and nethermost level of impurity. Had God waited any longer, had Moses extended his patience any longer, the result would have been irreversible, Israel would have fallen to an irremediable nadir, and the redemption could never have taken place.

Consider the revelation at Sinai itself. Jews were told to wait for three days. They heroically suppressed their curiosity and nervousness, and they waited. But they did it too well. They over-waited. They were so patient, that they were soon gripped by inertia, so that when the time came to respond, to show initiative, to climb, to ascend – they were fast asleep! And on the morning of revelation, the tradition teaches us, Moses had to go about the camp of Israel and arouse his slumbering people. Hence, as the author of *Magen Avraham* teaches us, we now have the custom of staying up all night on Shavuot to study the Torah to make up for that one fateful morning that we overslept (*Shulḥan Arukh, Oraḥ Ḥayyim, Magen Avraham* 494)!

So that waiting is good; but timely and precipitate action, such as the leap into the Red Sea by Naḥshon ben Aminadav, is even better. In this and in all else, we must follow the teaching of Maimonides about the "golden mean," the "way of the Lord" which bids us follow the middle path and yield to neither extreme – neither under-waiting nor over-waiting. Thus, waiting for the Messiah is a great Jewish virtue. To prematurely precipitate the redemption is the vice of impatience. But to wait endlessly and without any effort to create the circumstances and conditions for the Messiah, to leave redemption entirely in God's hands and to be totally passive in our waiting – this is a sign of quietism, of spiritual and political passivism. Had we followed this course, there would never be a State of Israel today!

We always confront the vexing problem of the balance between waiting too long and waiting too much. European Jewry in the 1930s and 1940s had that problem. It is too easy to don the mantle of self-righteousness and, with the benefits of hindsight and retrospect, blame the Jews of Europe for not getting out on time. They had a legitimate and excruciating problem: to wait longer to see what happens, or to abandon everything and get out quickly. There was a case when over-waiting had dreadful and deadly results.

Only two or three years ago, we in this country had the same problem with regard to Soviet Jewry. Some counseled us to wait longer. They made sense: impetuous action by American Jews in the public forum might very well endanger the lives, health, and substance of many Russian Jews. Others told us that if we wait any longer, we will have lost the opportunity to help them. It was a difficult decision to make. Most of us decided to wait no longer. The last two or three years have proved our decision correct. Thank God.

When the Israelites were told to wait before the giving of Torah at Sinai – as though waiting were a prerequisite to Torah living – they were told to wait until the shofar sounds: "When the ram's horn sounds long, they shall come up to the mountain" (Exodus 19:13). The Aggadah tells us that this shofar was no ordinary one. The shofar that sounded at Sinai was quite ancient. As Rashi quotes the Rabbis, it came from the ram that was substituted at the last minute for Isaac in the sacrifice of the *Akeda* that Abraham was commanded to make at Mount Moriah.

What does this mean? What is the relationship between these two events bound together by the one shofar? Nachmanides was puzzled and resorted to a mystical interpretation. Permit me to offer my own explanation. Abraham at Isaac's *Akeda* too had a three-day wait command to him – it was three days from the time he was commanded until he arrived at Mount Moriah. Abraham could have been over-tense, anxiety-ridden, rushing to get on with the job and get it over with, lest the wait of three days prove unbearable because of his love for his son. Had he done so, he would have killed Isaac, and there would be no Jewish people today. But he also could have over-waited, he could have stalled, hoping that his procrastination would defer the divine decree and he would never have to offer up his son. Had he done so, there never would have been an *Akeda*, and he would never have had the opportunity to demonstrate his heroism for God. Then we would have had a people – but it would not have been a Jewish people!

The shofar at Sinai thus explains the three-day wait before giving of Torah. The *hagbala* is, as Abraham taught, a lesson that we must yield neither to impulsiveness nor to endless procrastination. And as with Abraham, so with the Torah given at Sinai, and so with Jewish life which must always be co-extensive with Torah.

So we are not given any clear guidance that can serve us as objective criteria for each and every individual case. A man has no choice, in his own situation, but to call upon the resources of his own wisdom and judgment. But we are given guidelines. We are told the outer parameters in which we should form our judgment. At first, wait. Do not rush recklessly. If you have not waited at all, you are probably making a mistake. (A friend of mine who is a successful businessman in New England once told me that he never accepts any offer which requires an immediate response and does not permit him to think it through.) But then, beware of waiting too long. When you have waited, and you begin to feel the creeping paralysis of resignation, when you feel comfortable in your inertia, when you feel self-righteous about your waiting and suspect that it has become the substitute for action, begin to rethink your position.

The decision of to wait or not to wait; to know when an act is premature and precocious, and when further delay is deadly and irreversible – such decision is an agonizing one. It taxes the deepest resources of wisdom and intuition of even the leader – who must be neither a member of the "Now Generation," nor of the "Never Generation."

A man needs all the advice and help he can get, all the wisdom and experience he can muster, when he is called upon to walk the thin line between impatience and the paralysis of inertia, between impetuosity and procrastination. And even then, he needs divine guidance.

"They also serve who stand and wait," wrote John Milton in one of his sonnets.

"All things come to those who wait," Rabelais assured us.

And an English poet of the last century, Marie Montgomery Singleton, pondered this sage advice, took exception to the blanket generalization, and concluded:

> Ah, "all things come to those who wait"
> (I said these words to make me glad),
> But something answered, soft and sad,
> They come, but *often come too late*.

Seventeen
How Do You Know You're Awake?*

THERE IS AN OLD, GRAPHIC YIDDISH EXPRESSION OF the sense of sad and wise weariness which translates to "life is but a dream."

Often, indeed, it does seem that life is nothing more than a dream! However, Rabbi Israel Salanter, the great father of the Mussar movement, commented on this expression as follows: "only if you sleep away a whole life!"

Indeed so! But – how do you know if you're awake?

Now, that sounds like a silly question, inviting even sillier responses. However, I do not mean it simplistically. Nor do I mean the question philosophically, for there were a number of philosophical schools in England and on the continent which questioned whether or not we exist objectively, and by what criteria we can judge that we actually exist, except in someone else's dreams.

Rather, I mean the question existentially and spiritually and psychologically: How do we know if and when we are alert, fully alive, totally conscious, engaged?

Alertness or insensitivity, being asleep or awake, are relative

* June 5, 1976

terms. I have met people going through the motions of life – the conversations, the pleasantries, the business, the professions – and yet I know for sure that they are asleep. In fact, I know people who I believe never have been awake!

So, how do you know if you're awake?

Permit me to offer a Jewish answer by referring to the morning blessings. The last on the list of these blessings is one in which we say: "Blessed are You, O Lord...Who removes sleep from my eyes and slumber from my eyelids." However, of all the blessings in this group, this is the only one that is not recited in isolation. That is why, instead of answering "Amen" after it, we proceed immediately to the next blessing, which begins: "And may it be Your will, O Lord our God and God of our fathers, that You habituate us to Your Torah..." These two blessings or prayers are treated as one. Why is that?

One answer is that we ought to intend to sleep well in order to have the strength to study Torah. The famous author of *Turei Zahav* (*Shulḥan Arukh, Even HaEzer* 25) says, in the name of Maimonides, that if scholars sleep in order to study, "they receive reward for their sleeping." This is a beautiful answer, but not completely satisfactory, for the question remains that the blessing is recited not on sleeping, but on awakening!

Permit me to suggest another answer, namely, that if we do not study Torah, if there is no "that You habituate us to Your Torah", how do we know in the first place that we are awake? Without Torah, we must always confront the basic question of what criteria we have to know that we are not really asleep. With *talmud Torah*, we know for sure that we are awake.

Hence, the blessing of "Who removes sleep from my eyes and slumber from my eyelids" is intimately connected with the request to God to habituate us to a life of the study of Torah. It is Torah which determines if we are in slumber or aroused.

In a general sense, I would say that the criterion of wakefulness is the ability to get out of oneself. It must be the most basic answer to all those who wonder if they really are awake, who are perplexed by their own persistent superficiality, who complain of the feeling that life seems to be passing them by, who worry that they seem to be skimming over the surface of life like some excellent but unwilling water-skier, who never seem to taste deeply of the cup of life.

The egocentric, the narcissist, the boy or girl or man or woman lost in daydreams, always feeding his or her own ego, caught up in reveries of self-indulgence, is asleep, at most semi-conscious. It is only when you get out of yourself, when you are engaged with others, that you can consider yourself awake.

When that famous boat was sinking and all the passengers except Jonah were praying, the captain rightly reproached Jonah with the famous and sharp words, "what are you doing sleeping?!" (Jonah 1:6). He should have done as the others did – be concerned with the safety and security of his fellows, but instead he was not. One who is involved only in himself is a somnambulist who may give the illusion of being awake, but really is not.

It is not easy to stay awake. As a speaker, I know that as a persistent fact and a professional challenge. You need something to pull your interest away from dead center – namely, yourself – and activate it, and engage it to some great cause or compelling ideal or transcendent goal or profound love. And what is it that, for the Jew, combines all these things – cause, ideal, goal, love? Clearly, it is Torah.

That is why the tradition teaches us that there is a custom to study all night on Shavuot and not to sleep – and I am pleased that about 100 people did so here at The Jewish Center this Shavuot – in order to make up for a rather startling occurrence. That is, that the People of Israel, who used to get up at the crack of dawn in the desert of Sinai, slept late on the morning that they were to receive the Torah at Sinai. God had to wake them with thunder and lightning, a kind of celestial alarm clock. So, tradition informs us of the relationship of sleep and Torah – that they are in contrast with each other!

How, then, shall we keep ourselves awake, alive, and engaged, according to the Torah?

First, the Torah teaches us that we are part of a continuum of generations and thus breaks the cocoon of our selfishness by forcing us to attach ourselves to the past. When we remember the relationships that link us to parents and grandparents, when we are forced to confront the fact that history was not born on our birthdays, then we can begin to avoid the moral drowsiness and psychological languor that comes from being an isolated monad. In this sense, *Yizkor* does more for those who remember than for those who are remembered. Second, to become alive and alert one must reach out to others, in the horizontal or contemporary sense, and assume responsibility for his fellow Jews.

Of God Himself, we are told: "Behold the Guardian of Israel neither sleeps nor slumbers, the Lord shall watch over you and be your shadow over your right hand" (Psalms 121:4). God's sleeplessness, His quality of alertness is expressed by His care and concern for others: He is the Guardian of Israel. So is it for us. If we wish to live fully, deeply, we must live for others as well as for ourselves.

As Jews, we must do that by responding to the call of UJA and Federation, especially on this weekend devoted to the "Mobilization for Survival" campaign. It is not enough merely to issue a deep Jewish groan and say, "the world is against us." Neither is it enough to take any momentary delight from the disunity of the Arab states – which at worst is only an illusion of good news for us, and at best, a deferral of the crisis. We must do something to help Israel defend itself, and to help it strengthen its own inner fiber.

Finally, we are back to our original statement: the study of Torah is the best way to be awake. Without it, life for the Jew is full of voids and vacuums, and life can be one long yawn occasionally interrupted by brief periods of semi-consciousness. But with the study of Torah, with the awareness of its summons and demands, its promises and consolations, its intellectual stimulation and moral challenge – we are fully and deliciously alive.

Permit me to offer an interesting historical footnote from my own research. There is an interesting literature about an odd phenomenon that is peculiarly Jewish: that of many saints and scholars who experienced creative ideas in the study of Torah during dreams, while asleep! Now, during the period which saw the emergence of Hasidism, we find two opposite views. The Gaon of Vilna tells us that Torah which is studied and achieved during one's sleep is not genuine study. The Hasidim had the reverse point of view: if you study Torah during your sleep, then that is proof that it is not genuine sleep! Either way, both agree that sleep and Torah study are antonymous, they are in direct opposition to each other.

So, on this Shavuot when we remember the revelation of Torah at Sinai, we must determine that we shall become "regulars" in the study of Torah. In that manner, we shall have good reason to thank the Lord in the words of the conclusion of that blessing, "Blessed are You O Lord, who bestows gracious lovingkindness upon His people" (*Berakhot* 60b).

Eighteen
On the Look-Out*

TWO MOUNTAINS LOOM LARGE IN THE HISTORY OF OUR people and the traditions of our faith. One is Mount Sinai, from which Moses came down with the Ten Commandments. The other is Mount Moriah which Abraham ascended in order to bind his son Isaac and offer him up as a sacrifice until God bade him stop at the last moment. Both these mountains are prominent in the history of the civilized world. And yet one wonders at the difference between them. One wonders, why, when it came to building the *Beit HaMikdash*, the Temple, it was Mount Moriah which was so honored and which became sacred in Jewish law and life, whereas Mount Sinai retains only historic significance but is of no importance religiously. Why is it that Mount Moriah has become the geographic center of Judaism, the place to which we turn in our prayers, and Mount Sinai is just another little hill in the great barrenness called Sinai Desert?

In the answer to that question lies a whole philosophy, the essence of the Jewish approach to God and the kernel of the Torah world-view. The answer, in fact, can be expressed in a parallel study of two historic personalities whose names are associated with these mountains. They are Moses and Abraham.

* May 28, 1955

The name of Moses is inextricably bound up with Sinai, and Abraham with Moriah.

Moses, of course, is the prophet par excellence of Judaism. He is the lawgiver and the man whom God chose to redeem Israel from Egypt. He reached the highest rung any man can ever hope to reach. But the early history of Moses is one of ease and facility. There are struggles, but not great struggles. There are difficulties, but no tormenting ones. He was a man who was chosen to lead and to prophecy, and his very birth was accompanied by signs of greatness. He was tending his flock in the land of Midian one fine day when he heard a voice call out of a bush, which burnt but was not consumed. It was the voice of God summoning him to his great role in history. It happened so suddenly, so quickly. It seemed that he just "had it in him." And when, years later, he assembled his people about the mountain called Sinai, they too seemed just "naturals" for the word of God. There is even a tradition that they slept late that historic day and had to be awakened to hear the Ten Commandments issued by the divine voice. With folded arms they stayed at the foot of the mountain, while the Torah was given to them. That is the character of Sinai – a passive awaiting of God's word. Man waits while God seeks him out.

Abraham represents the exact reverse. He was a precocious tot of three – or, according to Maimonides, a man of 43 – when he first conceived of the idea of one God. God did not reveal Himself to Abraham. But Abraham, having come to the conclusion that there must be such a personal transcendent God, began to look for God. He spent the better part of his life trying to reach him. He braved the ridicule and the mockery of his idolatrous society because of his queer belief in and search for an invisible God. Not once in many years did God make himself available to the searching patriarch. Only after many heart-breaking decades did the word of God come to Abraham: *lekh lekha....* and then he was 75 years old! It was a successful and vindicating venture, this search for God, but only because it was a search – difficult, hard, often frustrating.

But if this long search was a hard one, how much more so Abraham's trek up Mt. Moriah. Here he was, in his old age, a father of one son born to him in his late years. And now God had called upon him to sacrifice this son atop the mountain. His religious nature responded affirmatively at once. His humanitarian side rebelled. His only real son, the one and only to his old mother. And yet, torn by this inner conflict, Abraham climbed the mountain, every step filled with pain and foreboding with a fire raging in his soul. He climbed up to God, and he finally reached the summit – he was going to follow the Godly voice! And he did, until the angel ordered him to desist, and told him that he had passed the test. That is the character of Moriah – a powerful looking for God, a dynamic active search by man for God.

That is what accounts for the holiness of Moriah and the religious insignificance of Sinai. Holiness is not a generous gift bestowed by God on prima-donna souls. It is wrested from God by the sweat of the brow and the mighty wrangling of the heart. A Temple is not built by religious wall-flowers. It is sanctified by searchers, by men always on the look-out for God. That is why Mount Moriah is crowned by the Holy Temple, whereas Sinai has nothing Jewish associated with it; on the contrary, on its summit today there is a Christian monastery.

Those who pray carefully might sometimes wonder: we often refer to God as *Elokei Avraham*, never as *Elokei Moshe*. Why? Because it was Abraham, not Moses, who searched the harder. And *Elokei Avraham* means the God of Abraham in the possessive sense, that Abraham actually "owns" a part of God. Rabbi Joseph B. Soloveitchik offers an interesting halakhic explanation. The halakha discusses the case of one who finds an object in the street, an object of value but which has no identifying marks. In such case, the law is "finders keepers." But what is the legal reason for the transfer of the property from the previous owner to the finder? The reason, according to the Talmud, is *ye'ush baalim*, the fact that the previous owners (knowing that it bears no identifying marks) renounce ownership because they despair of its return. In the same way, so to speak, did Abraham become possessive of God. There was no one who had any prior claim on God. Men had despaired of reaching Him. There was *ye'ush baalim*. But Abraham went on the lookout. He searched for this Divine *metzia*, and he found Him; hence, *Elokei Avraham*, the God of Abraham. Abraham looked for God, and so God was Abraham's. But God was the one who looked for Moses and found him, and so he is known as *Moshe eved Hashem,* Moses the servant of God (Deuteronomy 34:5). Moses was found by God and hence belongs to God.

It was only long after Sinai, after the Tablets there delivered were broken, that Moses changed his approach to God, that he announced *"har'eni na et kevodekha"* (Exodus 33:18), God, I am out to discover Your glory. It was only then that Moses rose to his eminent position in the history of humanity.

It is the same in religion as in all life, except more so. You never get something for nothing. In Torah it is even deeper: you must work much harder, but the returns are much greater. Those who have not experienced true *simḥa shel mitzva*, the ecstatic joy of spiritual achievement, have not lived.

I sometimes wonder at some of our Jews. I wish they would take their business shrewdness into the synagogue proper, not only to board meetings. Which businessman would trust an agent who tries to sell him stock that supposedly requires very little investment, involves no risk and gives tremendous windfall profits, without a thorough examination? And yet, these same people, so circumspect in finances, come into the synagogue and expect to invest three or visits a year, no risks of spiritual creativity and hardship, and expect God to jump every time they snap their fingers, expect to be "inspired." There is only one difference. In business, such speculative fly-by-night investment can cost you your shirt. In religion, you can lose your soul. Torah does indeed offer terrific spiritual profits, but not without heavy capital investment – investment of your time and energy and faith and money and prestige. It requires being constantly on the look-out for God, being a Mount Moriah Jew, not a Sinai Jew.

I wish people would not come into this synagogue to "be inspired" as one goes to a show to be entertained or to a steam-room to be massaged. This is neither a theatre nor a service agency. The rabbi is not an actor, nor does he aspire to be a masseur. This is a workshop, a workshop of the human soul where you are both the artisan and the vessel, where God is both the boss who demands and the customer who must be satisfied, and where the rabbi is just another poor, hard laborer who merely seeks to give some friendly advice. No one can find God without looking for Him, and it is just that the synagogue is the best place to look.

It is told of the great Hasidic teacher, Reb Baruch of Meziboz that his grandchild once came crying to him, and complained that he had been playing hide-and-seek with friends, and that he was hiding but his friend did not come to look for him. "Ahh," exclaimed the Rabbi, "but God has the same complaint. No one comes to look for Him."

If we religious Jews had taken that to heart fifty and sixty years ago in greater numbers and with more enthusiasm, the State of Israel today might have more genuine Jewishness in it, in place of the offensive secularism which sometimes tears at the heart. If only we had known then that Messiah would not come looking for us if we remained with folded arms. Messiah comes only when he is sought out, when he is looked for. Only then does one find *athalta degeula*. The Hebrew song, *Yerushalayim*, has one beautiful refrain: *me'al pisgat har hatzofim shalom lakh Yerushlayim*, from the summit of Mount *Tzofim*, peace unto you, O Jerusalem. Those who know Hebrew know that *"tzofim"* comes from the word which means to look, to search out. Only when Jews will begin to look for Jerusalem with love and devotion, when they will put their lives into the striving for the City of Beauty will peace come unto Jerusalem.

If parents would understand this difference between Moriah and Sinai, between Abraham and the early career of Moses, they would not be satisfied with the pitifully little they give their children. Parents who are happy with a three-day-a-week education for their children are not providing them with the equipment with which to undertake the long and tough search for meaningfulness and holiness in life. Those who give their children a two-hour-a-week fling in things Jewish are not only not providing them, but I dare say are blindfolding their own children; if one of these ever finds meaningfulness it is sheer luck. Those parents who give their children full, maximum education, those who give them – let us not be afraid to say it openly – a good day-school education if it is available, they are the ones who help their children. That kind of teaching means providing children with spiritual binoculars in the search for God.

"And from there shall you seek the Lord your God, and you will find Him, if you will search after Him with all your heart and with all your soul. In your distress, when all these things come upon you" (Deuteronomy 4:29–30), when man is troubled by the sheer emptiness of his life, when he is worried and pained, when he feels caught in a vise and tossed about recklessly in the tempests of life, when in distress, then God calls out, seek God, look for Him, and you will most certainly find Him. "For the Lord your God is a merciful God; He will not fail you, not destroy you, nor forget the covenant of your fathers which He swore unto them" (Deuteronomy 4:31).

Nineteen
The Little Things*

IN THE BOOK OF VAYIKRA, IN THE PASSAGE WHERE THE Torah first mentions the major festivals of the year, we find the intrusion of a seemingly irrelevant verse, one which seems out of context in this list of great holidays. Our Rabbis already wondered at the fact that after the mention of Pesach and Shavuot, and before the mention of Rosh Hashanah, Yom Kippur and Sukkot, the Torah introduces an extraneous verse, one which seems to have nothing whatever to do with the *moadim*, or holidays. "When you reap the harvest of your land, you shall not remove completely the corners of your field as you reap, and you shall not gather the gleanings of your harvest; for the poor and the proselyte shall you leave them; I am Hashem, your God" (Leviticus 23:22).

When reaping the harvest, you may not reap the whole field, but must leave a *"pe'a,"* a corner of the field unreaped; and the *"leket,"* the gleanings of the harvest, the ears of corn which fell to the ground were to be left there. This *leket* and *pe'a*, the gleanings and the corner, were to be left for the poor man and the stranger, for the needy and the alien who have not their own fields.

Our Sages (Rashi on Leviticus 23:22 quotes *Torat Kohanim*

---

* May 25, 1958

23:175), contemplating the mention of *pe'a* and *leket* in the context of the holidays, ask: Why did the Torah see fit to mention *leket* and *pe'a* in the middle of the portion of the *moadim*, with Pesach and Shavuot on one side, and Rosh Hashana and Yom Kippur on the other?

Many answers have been offered to this question posed by the Rabbis. All of them are worthy of deep study. This morning, however, I invite you to consider what I believe is the intention of the Torah in this juxtaposition of the mitzvot of *tzedaka* (for *leket* and *pe'a* are really forms of *tzedaka* or charity-giving) and the festivals.

We live in an age which has an unusual flare for the dramatic and the spectacular. Our interests are directed almost solely to headlines and lead articles. The big things in life, the flashy glamors, they attract us, while the prosaic, everyday matters are regarded as too dull to merit our consideration. In an age of space travel, only that which goes farthest fastest is deemed worth discussing, and yesterday's missile is passé. As one wit in the Pentagon is supposed to have informed his subordinates concerning rockets, "If it works, it's obsolete!"

In this kind of world, only a daring rescue becomes a virtue, while a kind helping hand is worthless. Only a dramatic act of courage is worth emulating, not an unspectacular deed of generosity. And at the same time, only the violent acts of murder or pillage must be avoided, not the small sins which attract no public comment. In this kind of culture, we read the best sellers, but neglect the classic literature which does not strike us as sensational. We devour every new report about the mysterious Dead Sea Scrolls, even though some of us have yet to read through the far older and more important Bible for the first time. We have, in other words, decided to live on the peaks of life, and have neglected the fertile plains below.

And nowhere is this attitude more pernicious and more dangerous than when it comes to religion and religious observance. For here too are we inclined to bring our worship of the big and dramatic and spectacular. Here too we may emphasize the great acts and cavalierly dismiss the trivial, to stress the glorious breakthroughs of the spirit and demean the constant, slow struggle of the human heart and mind and soul to rise upwards. Thus do we American Jews tend to concentrate on the so-called High Holidays and overlook the less dramatic Shavuot – we call it a "minor" holiday – and certainly Shabbat. We hear of adult courses on "Customs and Ceremonies" which deal with the great turning points of life of birth and marriage and death, and which leave all in between forgotten and neglected. We begin to think that Judaism consists of *bris* and *ḥuppa* and *shiva*, but that we may ignore such details as *tefilin* and *talmud Torah* and *taharat hamishpaḥa*, which are marked by quiet dignity and unobtrusive modesty. And it is to forewarn us against this concentration upon the big issues to the exclusion of the seemingly trivial that the Torah inserts the mention of *leket* and *pe'a* in between the great festivals of Judaism. Remember, the Torah tells us, that no matter how important the big holidays are, they are meaningless unless the Jew pays attention to the daily requirements as well, the simple things as *leket* and *pe'a*. Yes, the themes of the *moadim* are world-shaking – revelation on Shavuot, redemption on Passover, judgment on Rosh Hashana, repentance on Yom Kippur. Yet all of these lofty themes are for naught if the poor man remains outside, cold and hungry and forlorn, because you choose to neglect the prosaic and plain and paltry and petty mitzva of *leket* and *pe'a*. The great things are great indeed, the Torah means to tell us, but a man stands and falls on the small things. What determines the success or failure of the spiritual life of the Jew are not his grasp of the great theological concepts or even his participation in the synagogue festival service on High Holidays, but his everyday *leket* and *pe'a*, his daily Jewishness; not his rare splurge of kindliness as much as his constancy in *tzedaka*; not by his conduct in great public events, as much as by his *tefilin* and *tefila*, even in the privacy of his parlor, by his consideration for wife and children and neighbors, by his kashrut and his study of the Torah. In a word, the Torah counsels us to beware of the spectacular only and to concentrate as well on the substantial.

And oh, how history has proven the importance of the little things, the *leket* and *pe'a* amidst the *moadim*. The generation of Noah was destroyed by the flood because, tradition teaches, of *gezel pahot mishaveh peruta*, petty pilfering! The whole Egyptian exile began because of a mere two *sela'im* worth of silk which Jacob gave his favorite Joseph more of than his brothers, thus incurring their jealousy. The founder of Christianity began with a tiny sin – rejecting *netilat yadayim*. Reform started its career of truncating our *tefila* by eliminating only the *Yekum Purkan*.

Today we read from the Torah the *aseret hadibrot*, the Ten Commandments. There was a time, when the Temple was on Zion's heights, that they were recited daily as part of the service. Why do we not recite them thus today during our regular daily services? The Talmud answers that the Sages revoked this requirement, and actually forbade it because of *tar'omet haminim*, because of the heretics. They, the heretics, probably the early Christians, said they were going to observe only the big things, only the Ten Commandments, but that the rest was unimportant. Have you not heard that in our own day? "I'm religious enough; I observe the Ten Commandments." Aside from the fact that Shabbat is one of the Ten Commandments, and usually not observed by people who are satisfied with only ten of the 613 commandments, this is a typically Christian attitude. It plays up the big and dismisses the trivial. Murder, adultery, stealing are acknowledged as evils. But what of the minor sins; what of this willful ignorance of Judaism? What of this unJewish diet and vocabulary and whole pattern of unJewish living? So what our Rabbis told us about the Ten Commandments that we read on Shavuot – that better not to read them at all if that is going to be all of our religion, that better no Ten Commandments if we are going to neglect less dramatic mitzvot, that's just what the Torah meant when after

Shavuot in the list of *moadim* it mentioned in the unglorious but extremely vital mitzvot of *leket* and *pe'a*. The Yiddish writer Peretz put it in his own way: no man ever stubs his toe against a mountain. It's the little things that bring a man down. So it is with us, friends. None of us will ever commit murder. But someone may casually wound the pride of a friend by a word of *lashon hara*. No one here will ever bow to an idol. But someone may deny a smile to a neighbor who is starved for friendship. No one here is going to rob a bank. But someone may neglect to provide the *leket* and *pe'a* for a needy family. And it is these unspectacular little things, rather than the giant themes of the *moadim* or Ten Commandments, which ultimately decide our fate. That is why such seeming trifles are of such concern to the halakha – for trifles make perfection – and perfection is no trifle.

Twenty
To Be a Ruth-Like Jew*

THE BOOK OF RUTH, *MEGILLAT RUT*, WHICH WE SHALL READ later today as we do every Shavuot, has come under very close scrutiny these past two years or so. It is the story, you will recall, of the woman Naomi whose husband and two sons died after the famine caused them to emigrate from Palestine, and found herself left with her two young widowed daughters-in-law. One of them left her for her non-Jewish parents. The other, also non-Jewish, Ruth the Moabite, pleaded with Naomi and won her consent to stay with her and throw in her lot with her and become Jewish. Ruth ultimately meets Boaz, they marry, and Ruth bears a son to make Naomi's older years happy, and four generations later, from this same Ruth, there is born David, King of Israel.

What these new writers on the Book of Ruth have to offer is mostly a complaint. Why, they argue, is this called the Book of Ruth in the first place? Ruth was a fine young lady, but after all the real heroism, the real depth of character and even of strategy is shown by Naomi, not Ruth. Such is the argument of Maurice Samuel, and now of Dr. Hillel Zeidman. Naomi is the heroine of this great and charming biblical narrative, and the Megillah should therefore be called *Megilat Naomi*, the Book of Naomi.

* June 6, 1957

And yet our tradition *has* called it the Book of *Ruth*, and it is she, more than Naomi, who shines as the great heroine of the story. Naomi and Boaz are both pleasant and even gigantic characters, endeared to history and beloved by the generations. But *the* heroine, *the* ancestress of King David – that is Ruth and only Ruth.

Why is that? Why did Ruth receive so much more commendation and praise than modern students of the Bible are willing to give her? Primarily *because* she was *not* a Jewess to begin with; *because* she came to this Jewish way of life as a novice, as a newcomer. Of Naomi, we expect a certain noble course of behavior. Of Boaz we expect a high-minded and noble attitude, for he was a great Jew and it was only Jewish to do what he did. But Ruth – not only did she voluntarily accept these ways and laws and beliefs and observances – but because of her very newness, because of her fresh perspective, she derived more from them and brought more to them. For Boaz and for Naomi a Jewish way of life is just natural; for Ruth it was an amazing adventure, a breaking open of new and thrilling horizons, filled with new and startling meaning and having unexpected and inspiring consequences. It is, precisely this child-like wonder, this feeling of perpetual newness and freshness of the Jewish ways that gave Ruth her superiority over the others. For her all that was Jewish and Godly could never become stale and routinized; it must always remain a new and profound and thrilling discovery. Only that kind of vigorous perspective and attraction could make her turn to her mother-in-law and vow her loyalty to this new way of life into which she so eagerly sought admittance.

Perhaps that is what one of the Rabbis of the Midrash meant when they offered a highly cryptic comment on something Boaz said to Ruth in their very first conversation in the fields. He said to her, "May the Lord recompense your work, and may Your reward be complete from the Lord God of Israel under whose wings you have come to take refuge" (Ruth 2:12). The

Midrashic Rabbi Chassa merely repeats the last phrase (*Ruth Rabba, parasha* 5:4): "for you have come to take refuge under His wings." What does this repetition signify? Simply this: that Ruth's greatness was that she *came* to Godliness from afar. And so God and Judaism had so much more meaning for her. Because of her previous distance was her present closeness so much more valuable. When a person is like Ruth and views the whole panorama of religious life with this feeling of newness and surprise and delight, then indeed *tehi maskurtekh shelema*, is his reward complete, is his religious experience wholesome and full and pregnant with significance. Because she *came*, was her reward *complete*.

This attitude of newness and discovery and delightful surprise comes to my mind especially when considering those of us, some even here today, who have only recently begun to live more fully Jewish lives. Take the matter of a kosher home. To most of us, it is an automatic affair, requiring no special consciousness of what we are doing and inspiring no new feeling or thinking. We feel that is what we should do, what Jews have always done, and so we do it, period. That is quite alright, but how much fuller a life we would lead if we always had the same reaction to our kashrut as do those who have only recently adopted the observance. They have come to it for a number of reasons – and this holds true for other observances as well, from shul-going to Shabbat to family life. There were children to consider, there was a deep yearning for higher meaning in life, there were discussions with a rabbi or parent or teacher or friend. What to some of us is a good habit, is to these Ruth-like people who have "come" from afar to dwell under God's wings a startling discovery always full of hidden surprises. A simple thing like kashrut offers new and untapped sources of meaning. This is a personal response to a personal request by God. Their voluntarily-accepted self-restraint becomes for them a living exercise in the love of God; their self-imposed discipline an act of holiness; their new convictions become for them constantly challenging and revealing experiences as the eternal impinges in the temporal and as God enters daily life in so many unique ways. Food is no longer just food; it becomes fraught with great and overwhelming significance, because this is God's will that is being performed, and so all of life, every little aspect of it becomes important in the eyes of God. Can a man be insignificant if this is his life? Can he feel crushed or bypassed if whatever he does is important to God? His kashrut means that a greater spirit dwells in his home, a spirit greater than him and his family. His relations with his wife are therefore more delicate and considerate, more noble and more elevated, for God is there too. That is what happens when someone comes to kashrut from afar. Like Ruth, who came from afar, the reward is *shelema* – complete, there is much novelty and discovery in every aspect.

It is this delightful and refreshing attitude of seeing the familiar and the old as new and exotic that we who are religious must learn to develop for ourselves. That is why we read the Book of Ruth – yes, the Book of Ruth – on Shavuot, which commemorates the giving of Torah. All of Torah must be approached with this attitude. Twice a day, as part of our *Shema*, we say, "It will be that if you hearken to My commandments that I command you today…" (Deuteronomy 11:13). Why, our Rabbis ask (Sifrei Devarim 58:1), "today"? It was thousands of years ago, not today! And the answer given is "every day you read or hear these words, they should appear as new to you as if you had just heard them that day." Torah was given a long time ago. But we receive it every day afresh. Every new insight, every new experience, every new layer of meaning and understanding we penetrate is a new spiritual adventure, *a kabalat haTorah*. It is *hayom*, today – for it always appears ḥadashim, new and novel to us.

It seems that the truly religious Jew, the Ruth-like Jew, has something of the creative quality of the inventive scientist. The main quality of the great discoverer is not one who studies the exotic and extraordinary, but one who finds the unusual in the usual, the surprising in the commonplace. It is almost a child's world, and hence it is a childlike quality: to be intrigued by the everyday-ish, to be provoked by the commonplace, to be challenged and ever surprised by the ordinary. It is from this quality of wonder, of viewing the old as new and the familiar as strange, that the greatest discoveries of nature arise. And it is from this too that the greatest religious insight springs.

The German philosopher Kant once said that two things fill the mind with ever new and increasing admiration and awe: the starry heavens above and the moral law within. In our language we would say: the intricacies of nature and the marvels of Torah, God's World and God's Word. The world of nature, whether the starry heavens above or the dark deep of the ocean below, always appear *hadashim be'einekha*, new and filled with wondrous surprises, both for the scientific personality and for the religious personality. Our Bible, especially the Psalms and the Book of Job, is full of expressions of the wonder at the greatness of nature which is always startling and shocking in its greatness. But to this, the Jew adds: "the moral law within," that is, Torah and mitzvot, the Jewish way of life and observances and precepts. This too is a fascinating world where the more one ponders it the more revealing secrets does one uncover.

It was King David who expressed it most succinctly in his Sabbath Psalm: *"ma gadlu maasekha Hashem, me'od amku mahshevotekha"* (Psalms 92:6). "The deed" refers to God's creation, to Nature, and "Your thoughts," to Torah and the commandments. God's World and God's Word, the starry heavens and the moral order, both are continual sources of marvel. And no wonder King David understood this so well. For today, his *yahrzeit*, we read of his grandmother, Ruth, whose quality this was; for, coming from afar, she realized that to be a Jew means to dwell under the wings of God. For Ruth as well as for David, all the world was *hadashim be'einekha*.

To those of us who are, therefore, new to our Jewish practices, we say that not only do we admire you, but we envy you. And we want to emulate you. That is what the Book of Ruth urges upon the great majority of us – boredom and mechanical routine have no place in religion at its best. Better than nothing, most definitely. But not good enough. We must strive to be like Ruth, constantly challenged by new insights. Observances must become *ḥadashim be'einekha*, as if we had never done this before.

Those of us who are "regulars" at *daven*ing or in shul are sometimes apt to become over familiar with the synagogue and prayer book. And when they become commonplace and lose their novelty we begin to lose reverence. We talk during *davening*, we act lightheartedly and feel called upon to demonstrate our sense of humor when we should be experiencing wave after wave of surprise and amazement emanating from the new – always, always new – words and ideas of that treasure-chest of meaningfulness called the Siddur. Our Talmudic Sages spoke often of *ḥiddush betefila*, of new ideas, new experiences and novelties of all kinds in our prayer. The same words, the same passages, the same motions, but completely new prayers nonetheless. The words, the books, the prayers – the very synagogue building itself – must always appear as a challenging newness to us.

But if this thoroughly Jewish attitude, so well exemplified in the life of Ruth, is to be brought to bear on the inanimate world of nature and to the observance of practical mitzvot, how much more so should this attitude be brought to our relationships with our fellow men. For people – humans – are God's greatest creation in nature, and one of the very greatest mitzvot is the love of our fellow men: *Ve'ahavta lere'akha kamokha* (Leviticus 19:18).

All too often we take people for granted – husband, wife, parents, in-laws, colleagues, friends, neighbors – anyone. We accept their opinions, fears, likes, prejudices at face value, and feel we know all there is to know about them. We no longer look for new experiences of friendship and interhuman discourse. We take them for granted and grow bored. We act as if their behavior is completely predictable, thus making of them mere machines. Well, it just isn't so. We must learn to scratch below the surface and be amazed by the new surprises and new facets of character, new insights into old friends' characters. The human personality is one of the most tantalizing mysteries on the face of the earth. To be challenged, provoked and inspired anew by it every day – that is the intelligent, Jewish, Ruth-like way. To ignore it, take it for granted and skim over it superficially – that is the foolish and cruel and Ruth-less way. It is only when a man is constantly attracted by the surprising depth of his neighbor's character and personality that he can become Ruth-like and observe *ve'ahavta lere'akha*. Otherwise, he must fail to observe that great mitzva and remain Ruth-less. Nature, mitzvot, people – all must always appear *ḥadashim, ke'ilu shematem hayom*.

It was this quality of Ruth's, of finding new sources of meaning and surprising depths in every deed and person, that lead her to turn to her mother-in-law with such fierce and yet tender loyalty. Certainly, the more expected thing for a young woman only recently widowed would have been to leave Naomi. Certainly, one would expect that Naomi symbolized for her an alien people into which she unfortunately married, that Naomi would be to her a symbol of her tragic past, of her failures, of her widowhood of her suffering and that she would be only too glad to take her leave of this prematurely old dominating character as quickly as possible. Yet she doesn't. She has brought her childlike wonder to bear to her mother-in-law. She has found new discoveries in this woman. She has become attracted to her. She loves her enough now to issue that immortal declaration, "where you go, I will go; where you lodge, I will lodge; your people shall be my people; and your God, my God; where you die, I shall die, and there will I be buried" (Ruth 1:16). Only that person can say that to whom others always appear ḥadashim, new, though you've known them a whole life long.

No wonder that Hasidim taught that every mitzva has its own individual *neshama*, its own soul. For that *neshama* is the repository of untold surprises, of amazing facets and abilities and meanings, it is the treasure-house of secret ideas and mysterious experiences, both of a mitzva and of a human being. "How great are Your deeds O Lord!" (Psalms 104:24), Your natural creations, and how deep Your thoughts, Your mitzvot – and how inscrutably magnificent is the human being, the greatest of both Your deeds and Your thoughts!

On this Shavuot, therefore, we are asked to develop that divine capacity for looking at our world, at our Torah and at our fellow human beings as ḥadashim, as delightfully new and always filled with amazing dignity and meaning. Having done that, having acted as if we had first heard the word of God this day, today, as if we had come from afar, as if this is our first drink from the cup of spiritual joy we will be protected by the wings of God as our complete reward. For a Ruth-like generation cannot long remain Ruth-less.

Twenty-One
Who Is the Missing Relative?*

THE BOOK OF RUTH READ ON SHAVUOT IS A BEAUTIFUL and inspiring story, instructive to us in many ways. The story itself is fairly simple, and most of us are, or should be, well acquainted with it. The cast of characters is well-known: Boaz, Ruth and Naomi as the major characters, and Orpah, Elimelekh, Mahlon and Khilyon as the minor characters.

But there is one personage who makes a brief appearance in this Book whom we may designate as the "Mystery Man." The Bible doesn't even give him a name. He is an anonymous and therefore mysterious character. You recall that Boaz was determined to marry this young widow of his cousin, this Moabite girl Ruth who had embraced Judaism. Now since Ruth and her mother-in-law Naomi owned the land left to them by their husbands' marriage, that would mean that these lands would be transferred to the new husbands. Let us remember that in those days real estate had more than commercial value; it meant the family inheritance, and sentiment was supported by law in making every attempt to keep property within the family or as close to it as possible. Now while Boaz was a first cousin,

* May 17, 1956

there was a nearer relative, the brother of Elimelekh who was the father of her late husband. Before Boaz could marry her and take possession of the family property, he must have the closer relative's consent (this relative is called the *go'el* or redeemer, for he redeems the family's possessions). Boaz therefore met this man, offered him priority in purchasing the lands of father and sons. He seemed willing to do this, regardless of price. But when Boaz told him that he would also have to marry Ruth if he should redeem the land, this *go'el* hesitated, then refused. I can't do it, he said. Boaz was then next in line for the right of redemption, and that he did, and, of course, he married Ruth too and from them, four generations later, came one of the greatest Jews who ever lived, King David.

Who is this relative who missed the opportunity of his life? What is his name? We do not know. The Bible does not tell us. It does tell us rather pointedly that it does not *want* to mention his name. In describing Boaz's calling to him to offer him the chance of redemption, we read, "*Vayomer sura, sh'va po, ploni almoni*, And he said, come here, such a one, and sit down" (Ruth 4:1). *Ploni almoni*, such a one. Lawyers might translate those words as "John Doe." Colloquially, we might translate those words as "so-and-so," or the entire phrase in English slang would read, "And he said, hey you, come here and sit down." Translate it however you will, the Torah makes it clear that it has no wish to reveal this man's name. Evidently, he doesn't deserve it. He isn't worthy of having his name mentioned as part of Torah.

And we may rightly wonder at the harsh condemnation of this person by the Torah. Why did he deserve this enforced anonymity? He was, after all, willing to redeem the land of his dead brother and nephew. But he balked at taking Ruth into the bargain as a package deal and marrying her out of a sense of duty. Well, who wouldn't do just that? Are those grounds for condemnation? As a matter of fact, our Rabbis tried to pry behind this veil of secrecy and they found his true name. It was, they tell us, *Tov*, which means good. He was a good chap. He showed a general good nature. There was nothing vicious about him. And yet the Torah keeps him as a mystery man, it punishes him by making him a nameless character. He remains only a faint and anonymous shadow in the gallery of sacred history. His name was never made part of eternal Torah. He was deprived of his immortality. He is known only as *ploni almoni*, "the other fellow," "so-and-so," "the nameless one." A goodly sort of fellow, yet severely punished. Why is that so?

Our Sages have only one explanation for that harsh decree. By playing on the word *almoni* of the title *ploni almoni*, they derive the word *ilem* – mute or dumb – *shehaya ilem bedivrei Torah*, he remains without a name because he was mute or dumb, speechless in Torah (*Ruth Rabba, parasha* 7). He was not a Torah-Jew. Some good qualities, yes, but not a *ben Torah*. When it came to Torah he lost his tongue. He could express himself in every way but a Torah way: *ilem bedivrei torah*. Had he been a Torah kind of Jew, he would not have sufficed by just being a nice chap and buying another parcel of land. He would have realized that it is sinful to despise and underrate another human being merely because she is a poor, forlorn, friendless stranger. Had he been imbued with Torah he would have reacted with love and charity to the widow and the orphan and the stranger, the non-Jew. Had he ever bothered to study Torah, as a Jew should and must, he would have known the elementary principle of *Moavi velo Moavit*, that once this Moabite girl had decided to embrace Judaism from her own free will and with full genuineness and sincerity that she is as thoroughly Jewish as any other Jewess and that one may marry her as one would the daughter of the Chief Rabbi of Israel. But this man was *ilem bedivrei torah*, he was unfeeling in a Torah way, he was out of joints with the spirit of Torah, he was ignorant of its laws and teachings, he had no contact with it. And a man of this sort has no name, insofar as Torah is concerned. He must remain *ploni almoni*, the nameless one. Such a person is unworthy of having his name immortalized in the Book of Eternal Life. His name has no place in Torah.

What we mean by "a name," therefore, and what the Torah meant by it is something infinitely more than the meaningless appellative given to a person by his parents. It refers, rather, to a spiritual identity, it is the symbol of a spiritual personality in contact with the Divine, and hence with the source of all life for all eternity. A name of this kind is not given; it is earned. A name of this sort is not merely registered by some bored clerk in the city records. It is emblazoned in the sacred letters of eternity on the firmament of time. One who is, therefore, *ilem bedivrei Torah*, strange to Torah, can never be worthy of such a name. He must remain a *ploni almoni*.

It is told of the famous conqueror, Alexander the Great, that he was inspecting his troops one day and he spotted one particularly sloppy soldier. He said to him, "Soldier, what is your name?" The soldier answered, "Sir, it is Alexander." The great leader was stunned for a moment, then said to him, "Well, either change your name or change your behavior." That is what we mean by a name in Torah. It is the behavior, the personality, the soul, and not the empty title that counts.

As far as we Jews are concerned as a people, we can be identified in no other way than through Torah. Without it we are a nameless mass. Without Torah there is assimilation, and Israel no longer exists. Our history, like that of other peoples, has in it elements of military ventures, politics, economics. But more than any other people, it is a history of scholarship, of Torah. It was a non-Jew – Mohammed, the founder of Islam – who called us "The People of the Book;" not just books, but "The Book". It was a non-Jew – the famed economist Thorsten Veblen – who called Jews "eternal wayfarers in the intellectual no-man's land." It was a non-Jew – the Protestant philosopher Paul Tillich – who said that for Christians, Jews serve the spiritual purpose of preventing the relapse of Christendom into paganism. It was a non-Jew – the King of Italy – who in 1904 told Theodor Herzl that "sometimes I have Jewish callers who wince perceptibly at the mere mention of the word Jew. That is the sort I do not like. Then I really begin talking about Jews. I am only fond of people who have no desire to appear other than they are." The King of Italy was referring to nameless Jews, those who reject the name "Jew," those who are "mute in the words of Torah." For the Jew who is not *ilem bedivrei torah* knows that the function and destiny of our people is to be a "holy nation and kingdom of priests." As a people we have the choice: remain with Torah and be identified with the House of David, be *bnei melakhim*, princes of the spirit, or become nameless and faceless blurs in the panorama of history, a collection of *ploni almomi*s.

And what holds true for our people as a whole holds true for us as individuals as well. The Kabbala and Hasidism have maintained that the name of every Jew is *merumaz baTorah*, hinted at in Torah. Here too they meant "name" as a source of spiritual identification, as an indication of a living, vibrating, pulsating, soulful personality, a religious "somebody." When you are anchored in Torah, then you are anchored in eternity. Then you are not an indistinguishable part of an anonymous mass, but a sacred, individual person.

We who are here gathered for *Yizkor*, for remembering those dearly beloved who have passed on to another world, we should be asking ourselves that terrific question: will we be remembered? How will we be remembered? Or better: will we deserve to be remembered? And are we worthy enough to have our names immortalized in and through Torah? Are we or are we not *ilemim bedivrei Torah*?

Oh, how we try to achieve that "name," that disguise for immortality! We spend a lifetime trying to "make a name for ourselves" with our peers, in our professions and societies. We leave money in our wills not so much out of charitable feelings as much as that we want our names to be engraved in bronze and hewn in stone. And how we forget that peers die, professions change, societies vanish, bronze disintegrates and stone crumbles. Names of that sort are certainly not indestructible monuments. Listen to one poet who bemoans the loss of his name:

> Alone I walked on the ocean strand,/ A pearly shell was in my hand;
> I stooped and wrote upon the sand/ My name, the year, the day.
> As onward from the spot I passed,/ One lingering look behind I cast,
> A wave came rolling high and fast,/ And washed my lines away.

The waves of time wash names of this kind away, indeed. Try as we will, if each of us remains *ilem bedivrei Torah*, unrooted in Judaism, then we remain as well *ploni almoni*. Is it not better for us to immortalize our names in and through eternal Torah, so that God Himself will know us other than as *ploni almoni*?

There is a custom which we do not practice but which Hasidic congregations do, which throws this entire matter into bold relief. The custom stems from the famous Shlah HaKadosh who recommends that in order that our names not be forgotten on Judgement Day, that we recite a verse from the Bible related to the name at the end of the daily *Shemoneh Esrei*. There is a biblical verse for every name. Thus, my own is Naḥum, and the verse I recite is from Isaiah (Isaiah 40:1), "*Naḥamu naḥamu ami yomar Elokeikhem*, Console, console My people, says your God." My, what that makes of an ordinary name! Even as a child I was terrifically impressed with it – a job, a mission, a destiny: console your fellow men, your fellow Jews! Let any man do that and no matter what his parents called him, God knows his name – it is not *ploni almoni*; it is an eternal verse which will be read and taken to the hearts of men until the end of days.

On this *Yizkor* Day, think back to those you will shortly memorialize: does he or she have a name in Torah – or must you unfortunately refer to *ploni almoni* – a shadow of a memory about to vanish? How will we be remembered – not by children, not by friends, not by other men at all – but at on the Day of Judgement, by God Himself? Will we distinguish ourselves with humility, so that our names will become merged with the glorious verse of Micah (Micah 6:8): "walk humbly with your God?" Or will we prove ourselves men and women of sincere consideration and kindness and love for others so that our names will be one with *Ve'ahavta lere'akha kamokha?* (Leviticus 19:18) Or will we devote our finest efforts to the betterment of our people and effecting a rapprochement between Jews and their Torah, so that our names will be *"Beni bekhori Yisrael –* Israel is my firstborn" (Exodus 4:22)? Will we delve to the limits of our mental capacity into the study of Torah, so that our names will be found in *"Etz ḥayim hi lamaḥazikim ba* – it is a tree of eternal life to those that hold it"? Or will we do none of these things, just be *tov*, good-natured men and women with no special distinction in Torah, no real anchorage in Jewishness, and find that our lives have been spent in nothingness and that even God has no name for us, that we will be just plain *ploni almoni*?

On this Shavuot day, when we recall the giving of the Torah at Sinai, the "Mystery Man" of the Book of Ruth calls to us from the dim obscurity in which he has been shrouded: Do not do what I did. Do not be *ilem bedivrei Torah*, mute and speechless when it comes to Torah. Do not end your lives in a puff of anonymity. Grasp the Tree of Life which is Torah. Live it. Practice it. Overcome all hardships and express it in every aspect of your life. Do not abandon it or else God will abandon you. Jump at this opportunity for immortality. In short, make a name for yourself – through Torah, and with God.

Twenty-Two
Four Steps*

THE BOOK OF RUTH, WHICH IS READ ON THIS FESTIVAL of Shavuot, and whose mood of pastoral beauty at harvest time in the agricultural community of ancient Palestine dominates the whole atmosphere of this holiday, teaches us, quite incidentally, a profound lesson on the very nature of Torah and its tremendous significance in our daily lives.

Our Rabbis seem to have attached great significance to the tender parting scene of Naomi, Orpah, and Ruth. That Ruth acted nobly, selflessly and devotedly we know. Her reward – marriage to the great Boaz and grandmother of King David – was deserved and recognized. But what of Orpah, the woman doomed to become the grandmother of this foul Philistine, this Moabite who returned to her people. True she did not remain with Naomi, with the religion and the people she adopted when she married the ill-fated son of Naomi. But, after all, she did make some attempt, some offer, to remain with her mother-in-law. Did not she too, with Ruth, declare her willingness to accept Judaism? Does not this unfortunate person deserve some recognition?

Yes, our Rabbis answer, she deserved and got recognition. "R. Berekhia says that Orpah accompanied her mother-in-law four

* May 29, 1955

steps, and because of this kindness of four paces with Naomi, her descendant Goliath was spared for forty days between the time he challenged Israel and terrorized his Hebrew enemies and the time young David came and slew him" (*Ruth Rabba, parasha* 2:20). Only four steps, four small steps. But they were significant, they were important. And for it, her Goliath was awarded forty more days of life, glorious days for him and his family and his Philistines; forty days in which he shined as the great hero, as the unchallenged champion of the battlefield, forty days in which he basked as the supreme warrior of the Near East.

It is only a small incident in the Book of Ruth, only a small side-road off the main highway of history where and Ruth and Boaz lead to David and Solomon and the whole story of the emergence of the Jewish people. But that is precisely what the Rabbis wanted to tell us: that every little act is important. Nothing man does goes unnoticed. Every move he makes is filled with meaning and real importance.

Perhaps that is one of the main contributions of the whole Bible. The Torah called upon man to realize the tremendous implications of simple acts. Not only do the "heavens declare the glory of God" (Psalms 19:2), but the simple deeds of men may either declare or deny that glory.

How insignificant those four steps seem! Why, right afterwards, according to Jewish legend, that same night that Orpah left Naomi she returned to her previous way of life, she plunged into a life of shame and sin, a life of degeneracy and promiscuity. And yet, they were great steps. They were meaningful. For how Orpah really longed to return to her home and her parents, to her familiar Moabite surroundings and routines, to her childhood idols and the relaxed looseness of her people, away from this life of trouble and anxiety and widowhood and bad memories of a husband she should never have married, and a mother-in-law who, no matter how pleasant, always remained a stranger to her, who had too many religious scruples, who believed in some kind of invisible God and was overly strict in her morals. How Orpah's heart pined and longed to leave this life of strangers and hunger and widowhood. How she awaited the blessed moment of departure, those wonderful words "I'm going home!" And yet she had enough sympathy and consideration in her heart to feel the bitterness of this woman who was her mother-in-law, the great void in her life, the terrible and overwhelming loneliness. And so Orpah did not leave her immediately, but walked with her – only a bit, mind you, only four paces. But four paces more removed from her own desires and dreams. A small act, terribly small, perhaps insufficient. But the Torah thought it important. God considered it great. And the reward was great – forty days of life and glory and victory. Certainly, simple acts have tremendous implications.

Many of you here this morning have probably been as frustrated as I, on occasion, when trying to convince others of the necessity for keeping the practical observances of Judaism. Try to "sell" kashrut or Shabbat observance to someone who is non-observant, and you are frequently challenged by the highly sophisticated question: "Do you mean to say that God is interested in such petty things? Do you think God cares about my diet or my dishes or whether and when I smoke or go shopping?" The question has been asked hundreds of times, and it really gives its own answer.

Of course, God is interested in what we call "small" things. If God were not interested in "small things," He would not have provided us with eyebrows, and we would be an ugly race; He would not have given us thumbs and we would be clumsy creatures. There is no such thing as a small thing in the eyes of God. And who knows but perhaps that the very reason, or one of the main ones, for many of these practical mitzvot is to teach us the tremendous implications of men's acts, simple though they appear.

The very fact that they have such great significance means that Man has some connection with God, an intimate one. It means that he is not a solitary creature on the face of the earth. "The Bible," writes Professor Heschel (*Man is Not Alone*, p.142), "has shattered man's illusion of being alone. Sinai broke the cosmic silence that thickens our blood with despair. God does not stand aloof from our cries; He is a pattern, not only a power, and life is a task, not a curse."

Surely that is one of the really great achievements of Torah. It endows with meaning and consecrates eating, drinking, marital relationships, the human word and the human thought, reading, walking, singing. A human being who know this does not lead an empty, lonely, desperate life. A man who knows – as our Rabbis phrased it allegorically (*Midrash Tanḥuma, Parashat Vayetzei*) – that every act of man creates either an angel or a demon, makes use of every moment and consecrates every act to a higher and nobler goal. Life is not dry and prosaic and utterly flat. It becomes deeper and higher and weightier, it becomes meaningful and three-dimensional and poetic.

Look at it this way, remember that four steps can account for forty days, and all of life assumes new meaning and greater significance and beauty. Simple things no longer seem so simple. A word becomes the echo of the silent oratory of the mind. A tear is the distilled drop of the turbulent emotions of the heart. A groan is the audible grinding of conflicting emotions and frustrated desires and hidden misery. A chuckle is the overtone of happiness from the orchestrated harmony of the whole human being. A scowl or sneer is a seepage or trickle of hatred from the heart when arteries of goodness have been hardened. A smile is the visible symbol of the goodness that lies within one, seeking to plant a seed of happiness and courage within another.

All these simple things come to be viewed like icebergs; one sees only a fraction of the topmost part, but the bulk is there, only hidden by the waters. And it is these simple things which can move mountains, which can kill and make alive, encourage and discourage. "*Da ma lemaala mimkha,*" said the Sages,

"...*ayin ro'a ve'ozen shomaat vekhol maasekha besefer nikhtavim.*" (*Pirkei Avot*, 2:1) With such knowledge, there is no longer such a thing as a "simple" act.

Every act of devotion becomes a profession of love, and every word of prayer a sacrifice. Every visit to the synagogue becomes a pilgrimage, and every memory of a dead parent a reverent consecration. The more we are concerned with God, the more is He concerned with us. That is why even the Orpahs in life are rewarded for a few steps in the right direction. That is why rabbis try to urge their people to practice Judaism, and why its abandonment shrinks one's outlook until even the greatest acts become arid and barren and empty.

It is told that when Henry Norris Russell, the Princeton astronomer, had concluded a lecture on the Milky Way, a woman said to him, "If our world is so little, and the universe is so great, can we believe that God pays any attention to us? It Dr. Russell replied, "That depends, madam, entirely on how big a God you believe in."

We believe in a God who is great indeed. To quote from the *Akdamut*, "He has endless might, not to be described even were the skies parchment, were all the reeds quills, were all the seas and waters made of ink, and were all the world's inhabitants made scribes." With a God who is that great, nothing is unimportant, and all is holy.

Appendix

*Scholarship and Piety**

Foreword

The center of the widespread discontent that has characterized the social and cultural transformations of the second half of the twentieth century into our own times is the university. It is not only that, as the habitat of young people, the campus has become the locus of rebelliousness, the place "where the action is." More significant, it is against the university itself, as the symbol of American education, that much of youth rebelled. It rejected the antiseptic disinterestedness of much of the irrelevant and pedantic academic exercises that substitute for scholarship. In the last decades of the twentieth century, and even to the present, it was repelled by that part of the academic community that has subordinated its goals to those of the military-industrial complex. And in the name of diversity, the scholarly "canon" of "dead white Europeans" was disdained.

However, if pure scholarship is dismissed as irrelevant, and industry or defense work is a case of "selling out," must the university necessarily commit its scholarly resources to those social and political causes that the most radical and vocal students demand?

The role of scholarship in contemporary society has not yet been defined with any finality. Much ink will yet be spilled before a consensus is achieved. However, until then, it is worth taking the

---

* This essay by Rabbi Lamm appeared as Chapter Eight of *Faith and Doubt: Studies in Traditional Jewish Thought*, by Rabbi Norman Lamm (New York: KTAV Publishing House, 3rd Edition, 2007). It is reprinted here with permission of Rabbi Lamm and KTAV.

trouble to learn how scholarship was viewed in another age and in another culture in its interaction with other values.

No pretense is here made as to the practical benefits of such wisdom. How traditional Judaism in the eighteenth century viewed the study of Torah as an intellectual exercise, in relationship to religious experience and piety, will tell us precious little about how mathematical physics or social psychology should relate to urban unemployment. But it will at least give us the reassurance that similar problems, mutatis mutandis, have engaged the most creative minds of the past. At least we are not alone in our vexation.

PIETY (*yirah, yirat ha-Shem, yirat ḥet, yirat shamayim*) is, needless to say, fundamental to all religion. It is, indeed, the characteristic mood and expression of religious man. In Judaism, however, there is a precept which challenges the supremacy of piety alone, but which is deeply bound up with it, and that is scholarship, specifically the study of Torah. The Mishnah considers this study as transcending all other commandments.[1]

The history of the prominence accorded to study as a major value in Judaism is beyond the scope of this chapter. Its culmination, however, came in the theology of R. Ḥayyim of Volozhin (1749–1821), as it found expression in his *magnum opus*, the posthumously published *Nefesh ha-Ḥayyim* and, to a lesser extent, in his weekly lectures on *Avot*, on which students' notes were collated and later published under the title of *Ruaḥ Ḥayyim*. Drawing upon the many sources of the halakhic, aggadic, and Kabbalistic traditions, R. Ḥayyim formulated his conception of Torah, and its corollary, the value of the study of Torah, for the most part in Kabbalistic terms. He assigned a value greater to Torah and its study than had ever been allotted or dared before. He saw Torah, in its hypostatic essence, as identified with divinity, and he located its origin beyond the World of the *Sefirot* – which the Kabbalah conceived of as mediating between God in His absoluteness (*Ein-Sof*) and the phenomenal world – and prior to the divine emanations of the myriads of mystical worlds. The source of Torah was not even *azilut*, the first of the four mystical worlds, the one in which God and His attributes constitute an indivisible unity and about which nothing can be said save that it exists and is known by such a name. Torah, said R. Hayyim, originates in the infinitely mysterious regions of the *Ein-Sof* itself and, therefore, is the *telos* of all existence. Not only that, but the continued existence of all the worlds, material and mystical alike, are contingent upon the study of Torah as well.[2] The question of whether the impetus for this rather bold assertion came in response to the challenge of the growing Hasidic movement and its implied threat to the supremacy of Torah and Torah study, or as an attempt to reestablish the prestige of scholarship in Torah in a country (Lithuania) where it had fallen into neglect, is a historical problem which is irrelevant to our present purposes. R. Hayyim was an educator, founder of the Yeshivah of Volozhin, and the leading rabbinic figure among the Mitnaggedim, who were the opponents of Hasidism, and so it is fair to assume that both tendencies joined in inspiring this response of the reformulation of the Torah concept. R. Hayyim's view deeply influenced the Yeshivah of Volozhin, which he established in the opening years of the nineteenth century, and through it all the other great academies of Lithuania, and subsequently in Israel, the United States, and England in the nineteenth and twentieth centuries and beyond.

In considering the problem of the relationship between scholarship and piety in the religious philosophy of R. Hayyim, and their relative evaluation, a further contribution by R. Hayyim to the concept of Torah study must be considered: his definition of the talmudic concept of *Torah lishmah*,[3] usually translated as "Torah for its own sake" – the motivation for the study of Torah. The definition of this teleology of study is determined largely by one's general orientation to Jewish values, such as the role of intellect as against ethical and ritual performances. Furthermore, the degree to which one insists upon pure motivation, that is, study of Torah *lishmah*, depends upon the significance one attaches to the study of Torah, as such, in the complex of religious values: the more one esteems the act of study relative to all else, the less is he disposed to demand *lishmah*, however one interprets the term, and to disqualify study in the absence of *lishmah* (i.e., *she-lo lishmah*); and conversely, the less one's relative emphasis on scholarship as a religious value, the more likely is his insistence upon *lishmah*.[4]

The various definitions of the term *Torah lishmah* can generally be grouped into three categories, it being understood that they are not mutually exclusive:

The Functional Definition: *Lishmah* means study for the sake of observing the precepts dealt with in the Torah texts being studied. Hence, *lilmod al menat la'asot*, to study in order to do, that is, perform the commandments being investigated.[5]

The Devotional Definitions: Torah must be studied "for the sake of Heaven";[6] for the love (rather than fear) of God;[7] or to attain certain mystical ends;[8] or to achieve *devekut* (communion) with God experientially.[9]

The Cognitive Definition: Study for the sake of knowing and understanding the Torah. In this definition, made famous by R. Hayyim, *lishmah* means *le-shem ha-Torah*, for the sake of the Torah itself.[10]

R. Hayyim's development of a cognitive teleology of Torah study as the essence of the concept of *Torah lishmah* presents a serious problem of the relationship of this cognitive intention or motivation to the functional and the devotional. Of these, the latter is the more troublesome. The functional aspect of the study of Torah is affirmed by all authorities in some measure and can readily be assimilated into any other interpretation, at least negatively: that one must never study not in order to practice.[11] At the same time, R. Hayyim's cognitive definition is not so involuted and exclusively reflexive and intellectualistic as to ignore the nonintellectual, functional significance of Torah.[12] Ratiocination is the key – true, the exclusive key, but only the key – to the mystical organism called "Torah," and therefore the other significations of *lishmah* are included in the complex of motivations in R. Ḥayyim's teleology of Torah study. The cognitive and the functional elements can therefore coexist; there is not necessarily any competition between them.

However, the question now arises as to the relationship between the cognitive (scholarship) and the devotional (piety) ends of Torah study. The latter, unlike the functional, cannot, by its very nature, be taken negatively. Is there, then, the possibility of a simultaneous teleology of the two? Are *ratio* and *devotio* compatible in the consciousness of the scholar? If not, how does R. Ḥayyim treat the latter, an obviously fundamental religious category, without jeopardizing the cognitive *telos* of the study of Torah? The problem – the relationship of scholarship and piety, the tension between the intellectual and the devotional in the study of Torah – has, as we shall see, both theoretical and practical consequences of the greatest importance.

The terms used by R. Ḥayyim to distinguish between these two poles are *Torah*, by which he means, of course, study[13] – the intellectual enterprise – and *Yirah*.[14] This latter term comprehends three related items in R. Ḥayyim's writings: the devotional experience (*devekut*), that is, the active, affective, ecstatic element in the religious devotion; the passive devotional mood or state of mind (the fear of sin, יראת חטא); and the study of the devotional or didactic literature (ספרי יראה, ספרי מוסר), which may or may not lead to the other two. While ultimately R. Ḥayyim deals with all three in like manner, in defining their relationship with "Torah" we shall, for analytical and historical reasons, treat them separately.

R. Ḥayyim's theoretical objections to *devekut*, Hasidic style, are important in his general criticism of Hasidism. His strictures mark him as the leading thinker among their opponents, the Mitnaggedim. His overall objections[15] are not germane to our problem. What is of relevance to us is his argument that an active, demonstrative religious experience simply cannot coexist with the emotional tranquility necessary for proper mental concentration and attention in the study of Torah *lishmah*, in order to understand.

In addition, R. Ḥayyim was personally suspicious of emotional extravagance,[16] a mistrust that seems to have been quite characteristic of Lithuanian Jews.[17] No doubt he was largely influenced in this respect by his teacher, R. Elijah, the Gaon of Vilna, who, despite his own charismatic gifts and mystical visitations, was highly skeptical of any demonstrativeness or boasting or any immodest publicity given to such intimate and private experience.[18] Neither in principle nor in personality was R. Ḥayyim, as a preeminently "halakhic man," favorably disposed toward the extravagant devotional experience of *devekut*.[19]

A quite different problem is presented in the relationship of the devotional state of mind, "the fear of sin," and the study of Torah. The preachment of this conscious piety was part of the public program of Hasidism. The mitnagdic rabbis (allowing for individual exceptions), following rabbinic custom, usually preached only twice a year, on the Sabbaths before Yom Kippur and Passover. The sermon on the latter Sabbath was confined to halakhic *pilpul* and rarely included moral exhortation, or *Musar*, which was left to the *maggid* or *mokhiaḥ*, the official preacher. The sermon on the Sabbath before Yom Kippur, the *derashah* for Shabbat Shuvah, was devoted to the preachment of *Musar*, especially by the greater rabbis, who often expressed annoyance at their colleagues who misused the occasion for a display of their talmudic virtuosity. Even then, their addresses were intellectualized and unemotional, and quite esoteric, making the greatest impression upon the inner circle of cognoscenti and often incomprehensible to the uneducated masses. The Hasidic zaddik, however, began to assume the functions of the *maggid* and, in keeping with the whole pietistic and "democratic" thrust of the movement, concerned himself with the inculcation of pious conduct and feeling (what R. Ḥayyim calls "the fear of sin"), which was preached every Sabbath, usually during the "third meal." Even when the zaddik employed the Kabbalah in his talks, they were exoteric, in comparison to the rarified intellectual discourses of his mitnagdic contemporaries on Halakhah. The Hasidic masters were conscious of the fact that their emphasis on this devotional mood was an innovation and, according to accepted rabbinic method, attempted to justify it. The reason they advanced for this emphasis was its necessity due to the diminished spiritual capacities of "these later generations."[20]

R. Ḥayyim, of course, does not deny the importance of piety; he unhesitatingly grants the need for *Yirah*, *per se*. "It certainly cannot be said, concerning the engagement in Torah, that there is no need for purity of thought and fear of the Lord; Heaven forbid!"[21] He quotes copiously from the Talmud, Midrash, and Zohar to demonstrate what is an obvious essential of Judaism, but a truism that nevertheless needs to be affirmed by him in view of his unprecedented emphasis on the intellectual dimension, that of the study of Torah. "Woe to scholars who engage in Torah but possess no fear of Heaven."[22] Hence "the priority of fear of the Lord is the major guarantee for the existence of the wisdom of the Torah."[23] On the basis of a passage in the Talmud,[24] R. Ḥayyim compares *Yirah* to the storage house and *Torah* to the grain to be stored therein. Without piety one simply lacks the capacity for study; if a man has not first prepared for himself the storage house of *Yirah*, then all his grain, that is, the *Torah* he studies, will lie on the fields and rot.[25] Thus, they are also coextensive: the greater is one's piety, the greater is the divine wisdom he can amass. *Yirah* represents the capacity for the study of Torah.

> It therefore depends upon the storage house of *Yirah* which comes first for man; if a man has prepared for himself a great storage house of pure fear of the Lord, then the Lord gives him wisdom and understanding in great abundance,

according as to how much his storage house can contain. All depends upon his storage space. But if a man has not prepared even a small storage space, i.e., he has no fear of Him at all, Heaven forfend, then He, in turn, grants him no wisdom at all, since it cannot endure for him, for his Torah becomes disgraced.[26]

R. Hayyim concludes his comments on the significance of the devotional state of mind for the existence of Torah in a manner that, at the same time, reaffirms the superiority of Torah over all else.

It has thus been explained that although *Yirah* is but one commandment, and the Jerusalem Talmud in the beginning of *Pe'ah* says that all the commandments are not equal to one word of the Torah, yet the commandment to acquire the fear of Him is very great, in that it is necessary for the major existence and survival of the Holy Torah, and without it [*Yirah*], it [*Torah*] becomes disgraced, Heaven forfend, in the eyes of people. Therefore it is necessary that it take precedence for a man over the study of Torah.[27]

Given this reverence by R. Hayyim for the devotional state of mind, and his prescription of its chronological priority to study, there emerges nonetheless one basic and profound difference between R. Hayyim and his anonymous opponents, the Hasidim. For want of a better term, and in the absence of any special nomenclature for the idea in R. Hayyim's writings, we may call it the "Dissociation Principle." Basically, the principle is this: whereas piety is certainly a commendable virtue, and a necessary prerequisite for true scholarship in Torah, nevertheless, in contrast to Hasidism, the two must not freely intermingle. A clear line of demarcation must be set which will prevent interference of one by the other (specifically, *Torah* by *Yirah*), preclude conscious interpenetration of the two, and keep the domains of the mind and the spirit separate. Thus

while the total personality of the Jew possesses, conterminously, both the elements of *ratio* and *devotio*, as a desideratum or ideal, the two must be kept separate and distinct as conscious endeavors in a strict compartmentalization.[28] The Dissociation Principle is applied by R. Ḥayyim only to the study
of Torah and not to the performance of the other commandments. This distinction flows from, and guards his own position against, his strictures on Hasidic *devekut* during the time of study.[29]

It is precisely because *Yirah* cannot be practiced simultaneously and concomitantly with *Torah*, as it can with other *mitzvot*, that a more detailed analysis of the relationship of scholarship and piety is called for. Some of this exposition by R. Ḥayyim has already been mentioned; thus the chronological priority, despite the axiological subordination, of *devotio* to *ratio*.[30] A corollary of this separateness and inequality in value of the two elements is R. Ḥayyim's insistence that the devotional mood not be fostered at the expense of scholarship. Referring again to the metaphor of storage house and grain, and basing this upon the same Talmudic passage,[31] R. Ḥayyim puts the issue directly and quite strongly:

> So it is in the matter of *Yirah*: if one spends more time on it than is necessary for the preservation and survival of the abundance of grain, i.e. Torah, then he is considered to be robbing the Torah of that extra time which he should have been spending in study. For it was not permitted to engage in the contemplation and acquisition of *Yirah*, except as one can estimate intelligently that, in accordance with his own nature and condition, this is the amount of time that is needed, and necessary for him, to engage in the acquisition of *Yirah* and *Musar*, for the purpose of the preservation and survival of the grain of Torah.[32]

The conscious meditation in "the fear of sin" is, furthermore, especially superfluous for the true student of Torah, because the man who regularly studies Torah *lishmah* does not need all this toil and exertion and long time spent on books of *Yirah* as does one who does not regularly engage in Torah.

> For the holy Torah of itself invests him with the fear of the Lord in very little time and with very little effort expended on it. For this is the way and peculiar quality of the Holy Torah; as [the Rabbis] said (*Avot* 6:1), "whoever occupies himself with the study of Torah *lishmah*... [the Torah] invests him with humility and fear."[33]

Moreover, not only does erudition in Torah inspire conscious piety, without special efforts made toward that end, but the study of Torah is itself a form of objective *devekut* in the Torah, so that the very act of intellection in Torah is, by and of itself and without any awareness of devotional intention, an act of piety.

> During the study of and inquiry into Torah one certainly does not need *devekut* at all, for by means of study and inquiry alone one is attached (*davuk*) to His will and His word, and He and His will and His word are One.[34]

R. Ḥayyim's identification of the study of Torah as itself an act of *devekut* is not original with him;[35] but in light of the supernal origin of Torah, according to R. Ḥayyim, the act of automatic *devekut* becomes accordingly more sublime. It is this same august, trans-*azilut* origin of Torah that accounts for the fact that R. Ḥayyim applies the Dissociation Principle only to study of Torah and not to the performance of the commandments; the latter, optimally, should be accompanied with *devekut*, in order thereby for one to achieve the proper mystical effects (*tikkunim*), but the study of Torah, the laws of the commandments and their *halakhot*, must be "for their own sake," that is, cognitively, for the sake of the very words of Torah, to know and understand them, unaccompanied by any other consideration.[36] The fact that study of Torah is in itself an act of *devekut* does not obviate the need for at least some time consciously to create a devotional mood; but the time so set aside must not be excessive:

> Therefore, in truth – and this is the true way which He, blessed be He, chose – every time before a man prepares to study, it is proper for him to meditate in pure heart before he begins, at least for a brief period, in pure fear of the Lord,[37] to confess one's sin from the depths of his heart, so that his [study of] Torah may be holy and pure. He should intend to attach himself [i.e., effect *devekut*], by means of this study, with the Torah, with the Holy One; that is, to attach himself [i.e., effect *devekut*] with all his powers to the Word of the Lord, which is Halakhah. Thereby he will be attached [*davuk*], as it were, with God, in reality; for He and His will are One, as the Zohar states. And every law and Halakhah of the Holy Torah is His will, for thus did His will decree, that this be the law: valid or invalid, impure or pure, forbidden or permitted, guilty or innocent. Even if he studies the words of the Aggadah, which are irrelevant to the law, he is also attached [*davuk*] with the word of the Holy One … and He and His word are One.… Therefore all the Torah is uniformly sacred without any difference or change at all, Heaven forfend.[38]

However, R. Ḥayyim repeats more than once, this time put aside for nurturing the devotional mood, "fear," must not be disproportionate to its importance relative to Torah. Thus, referring again to the talmudic passage in *Shabbat* 31a, R. Ḥayyim takes the Aggadah in utter literalness[39] and therefrom deduces that if we calculate fifteen hours per day devoted to the study of Torah [*sic*(!)], then no more than about five minutes ought to be set aside for "fear,"[40] and, again taking a text – this time a mishnah[41] – literally, places this five-minute devotional period at the very beginning of the day. Nevertheless, he adds, study remains supreme, for piety is but the "storage house," contrary to those who, holding piety to be more important than scholarship, ridicule those who study Torah declaring that they study *she-lo lishmah*.[42] As a maximum, R. Ḥayyim would allow an additional brief period in the middle of one's studies for devotional meditation, if one feels that his "fear of the Lord" is weak and will not endure.[43] He apparently feels that doing this will not violate the Dissociation Principle provided it is not overdone and the period for "fear" is clearly delineated so that it does not interfere with the exclusive mental concentration necessary for proper study of the Halakhah.[44]

What does this devotional meditation consist of? The "accounting with his Owner in purity of heart in fear of the Lord"[45] comprises three distinct elements. The first of these is the cleansing of oneself from past transgressions by means of thoughts of repentance.[46] The second is the awareness that the purely intellectual study of Torah in and by itself constitutes *devekut* with the divine Word and Will.[47] Finally, the student must resolve to practice and observe all the precepts of both the Written and Oral Torah.[48] In a sense, we have here a résumé – although R. Ḥayyim does not explicitly state so – of the three major definitions of *lishmah:* the first recalls the devotional, the second, the cognitive definition of R. Ḥayyim (according to whom intellection is not an end in itself but the means to the organic mystical entity called Torah), and the last is, clearly, the functional.

The Hasidim, against whom R. Ḥayyim was reacting in establishing scholarship as superior to piety, disagreed, of course, with the views of R. Ḥayyim, but they were not altogether unaware of the problems he raised. Recognizing the fact that rabbinic tradition grants primacy to the act of study of Torah, the Baal Shem Tov (Besht) declares that in past generations, people were strong in "fear" and holiness and hence did not have to meditate in "fear," but since then a historical change has occurred, hence circumstances are different;[49] therefore, we cannot rely on our native predisposition to a devotional frame of mind and must set times for deliberate meditation.[50] The former emphasis on study is thus interpreted as operational or tactical, but essentially even study is subordinate to piety. Thus, extensive and uninterrupted preoccupation with study detracts from the greater good of piety, in the sense of God-consciousness. Constant meditation is necessary, for sometimes one can, by his very involvement in studying, increase the distance between himself and his Creator; hence, one must consider before whom he is studying.[51] *Devekut*, as a conscious, active experience, introduces an extraneous, nonacademic element into the mind of the student – a spiritual leaven according to the Hasidim, a pietistic distraction according to R. Ḥayyim.

The Besht does not have much good to say for the study of Torah in order to satisfy one's intellectual bent. Thus he asks: How can the Talmud refer to the halakhic discourses of Abbaye and Rava as a "small matter" (in contradistinction to the esoteric inquiry into Ezekiel's vision of the *Merkavah*, the basic text of much of the Kabbalah, which is considered a "great matter");[52] are not such discourses of the essence of Torah, revealed at Sinai? He answers that the Talmud does not mean to distinguish between the objective disciplines of Halakhah and Kabbalah, but refers rather to the subjective orientation of the student. Everything depends upon a man's intention. If his intention is merely cognitive, the comprehension of the subject matter, be it Halakhah or Kabbalah, it is "a small matter." "The discourses of Abbaye and Rava," that is, study for the sheer intellectual delight it offers, is almost of no religious significance; even if the subject matter is sacred, the act of study is not essentially different from the study of secular wisdom. If the motivation for study is, however, devotional, the achievement of *devekut*, then it is "a greater matter," for then one has indicated his willingness to make himself a *merkavah* for God,[53] whether it be through the study of Halakhah or Kabbalah or, for that matter, the performance of any *mitzvah*.[54] Clearly, then, the *telos* of the study of Torah is to be wholly devotional. It is in this spirit that R. Phinhas of Korets recommends that the student, in mentioning the opinion of any Tanna or Amora, try to visualize him as though he were standing before him, thus serving as an aid to drawing down upon himself the spiritual vitality that mystically inheres in the letters of Torah.[55]

The Besht himself recognizes an incongruity between the devotional and cognitive aspects of study and concedes the difficulty of doing justice to both simultaneously;[56] yet, he is not willing to grant the thesis that must have been cited in opposition to his outlook, and which was so persistently advocated later by R. Hayyim, namely that the study of Torah is in and of itself an act of *devekut* even without any special intention or spiritual effort. "Thou shalt be perfect with the Lord thy God" (Deut. 18:13) refers to the study of Torah; "perfect" means "study," as in the verse "the Torah of the Lord is perfect" (Ps. 19:8). Hence, even when you are "perfect," that is, engaged in the study of Torah, nevertheless you must be conscious of "being with the Lord thy God." Study without devotional intention is not considered dogmatically an act of *devekut*, of devotion or attachment to God. In an ingenious and characteristically Beshtian interpretation of a mishnah in *Avot*, he proceeds to expound his doctrine, according to which study may become an impediment to the achievement of man's spiritual goals; study without *devekut*, even if otherwise a man follow a straight path in life, is a case of his being alone, that is, Godless.[57] The direct Hasidic rebuttal to R. Hayyim, in the pseudepigraphic *Mezaref Avodah*, begins by granting the preeminence of *Torah* over *Yirah*, but then interprets the central prooftext of R. Hayyim's Dissociation Principle to diminish this principle and introduce, to a much larger extent, the periods of devotional meditation into the normal course of study.[58] To R. Hayyim's point that such meditation cannot coexist simultaneously with intellection because of its distracting nature, the author offers a psychological answer: granted that conscious thought of piety is disconcerting to the continuity of mental attention and concentration, nevertheless if the expanded program of devotional periods he recommends is followed, then this "fear" so acquired remains active on a subconscious level, and in effect we have a simultaneous act of study and devotion, one conscious and the other unconscious.[59] This position is patently a compromise between the pure *devekut* doctrine of early Hasidism and R. Hayyim's rigorous intellectualism.

What is the source of this approach of R. Hayyim to the relationship between scholarship and piety, between *ratio* and *devotio*? R. Hayyim's unwillingness to bend the disciplined activity of the intellect to, and even mix it with, the subjective flights of the devotional sentiments is probably in large measure a result of the influence upon him by the Gaon. Mention has already been made of the Gaon's and R. Hayyim's emotional quietude.[60] Yet the Gaon was a singularly creative Kabbalist, as is well known; his kabbalistic writings alone exceed in volume the sum of the output of all his Hasidic contemporaries,[61] and there was much, perhaps even more, that remained unpublished.[62] It should therefore come as no surprise to learn that the Gaon experienced mystic visions, though the extent and nature of these charismatic graces for a man of the Gaon's analytic acumen and extreme emotional sobriety are certainly astounding.

The main source for our information on this aspect of the Gaon's life is R. Hayyim himself, in his Foreword to the Gaon's commentary on the recondite Kabbalistic work the *Sifra de-Zeni'uta*. R. Hayyim infers from something the Gaon told him that he, the Gaon, experienced mystical visions ("elevations of the soul") every night since he arrived at maturity; a fellow student told R. Hayyim that he had heard this explicitly from the Gaon.[63]

In the Gaon's manuscripts, R. Hayyim read of mysteries revealed to the Gaon by Jacob, Moses, and Elijah. R. Hayyim is sure that the Gaon had nocturnal mystical flights but is not certain whether or not he experienced such visions while awake during the day as well. The conversations between the two, as reported by R. Ḥayyim, border on the incredible and would so be regarded were it not for the unimpeachable integrity of R. Ḥayyim. Thus the Gaon, in response to a direct question by R. Ḥayyim, related that he had already begun to create a *golem* by kabbalistic means, when something occurred which he interpreted as a sign from Heaven to desist because of his youth – he was not yet thirteen years old![64] The Gaon told R. Ḥayyim of visitations by angelic messengers called *Maggidim* – a term that covers a wide range of charismatic experiences[65] – who offered to reveal knowledge of Torah, ostensible halakhic information, without any effort or exertion on his part.[66] The Gaon had no use for learning gained so effortlessly,[67] not only because he doubted the authenticity of the information so imparted, as did R. Ḥayyim Vital in writing of the *Maggid* of Karo,[68] but because the lack of mental toil and labor invalidates the whole intellectual enterprise and condemns the results as worthless, even if correct.[69] The Gaon warned his students against them. R. Ḥayyim writes:

> Our Rabbi [the Gaon] sent me to my younger brother, my senior in all virtues, the pious and holy Gaon R. Shelomoh Zalman, may the memory of the righteous be a blessing, to command him in his [the Gaon's] name not to accept any *Maggid*-angel who will come to him, for in a short time such a *Maggid*-angel will indeed come to him.[70]

This left a deep impression upon R. Ḥayyim, who is reported by a student of his to have doubted, in the Gaon's name, the value of all these nocturnal visions which came to the Gaon without any of the conventional kabbalistic preparations, because they represented a form of reward, hence precluding full reward in the hereafter.[71] This "halakhic anti-supernaturalism"[72] may indeed, as has been suggested, be based upon the desire to safeguard institutionalized rabbinic procedures from the perils of charismatic anarchy,[73] but that is not the full explanation. We are, after all, dealing here with kabbalistic as well as halakhic information. His repeated references to the ease and facility with which such secret information is obtained[74] indicate that, in addition to any dangers that may flow from pneumatic lawlessness, the Gaon placed a special value on intellection *per se*;[75] he held that mental toil and effort are positive goods in their own right, and that they distinguish the intellectual enterprise from the emotional and charismatic life and hence must be kept rigorously separate from each other.[76] The Dissociation Principle, anticipated by the Gaon and fully developed by R. Ḥayyim, seeks to erect a wall of demarcation between the two domains not only in order to protect the Halakhah from being overwhelmed by the unpredictable and uncertain course of mysticism, but also to prevent the mind from being clouded by a fog of imprecise sentiment and thus cripple its analytic capacity,[77] and to guard against the infection of the halakhist-intellectual with the virus of indolence and the expectation of easy returns and great triumphs without investing the hard work and diligent exertion which are the absolute conditions of the valid intellectual enterprise.

Thus, the Gaon's valuation of intellectual effort transcends his concern for the independence of Halakhah from mystical aberrations and is cherished by him for its own sake. His counsel in this regard taxes human emotions as well as human energies. R. Joseph Zondel, a student of R. Ḥayyim, quotes the Gaon to the effect that determined men, resolute in their faith, will engage in Torah and *mitzvot* by day and by night, even if there is no bread in the house, and remain oblivious even to their children who cry for food; nothing will distract them from their labors in the study of Torah.[78] Acts of mercy that can be achieved without bother and worry and wasting time from the study of Torah constitute a great *mitzvah*, but only if they can be accomplished in the minimum amount of time and not divert one's attention from the study of Torah.[79] It is needless to add that the Gaon practiced what he preached in an exemplary and unique manner. His phenomenal concentration and superhuman diligence were the stuff of legends, as was his native genius.[80] The Gaon was extremely persistent, returning to the same subject "several hundreds of times" if necessary to understand it properly.[81] He reviewed his studies "a hundred and one times" several times over, and literally gave his life for every word and interpretation of Torah; his intellectual activity in the study of Torah was constant and uninterrupted.[82] R. Ḥayyim complains that he himself had not been blessed with the incredible and unimaginable diligence of the Gaon.[83] Certainly, then, the Gaon exerted a decisive influence over R. Ḥayyim in the latter's formulation of the role of the intellect in Judaism and, more specifically, the relation of *ratio* and *devotio* in the study of Torah.

Yet, R. Ḥayyim carried the Dissociation Principle even further than his master. The Gaon's chief concern was to safeguard Halakhah from being encroached by pneumatic *experiences*; but he did permit a symbiosis of Halakhah and kabbalistic *doctrine*, occasionally accepting the Kabbalah as the source of Halakhah, which R. Ḥayyim did not.[84] Despite R. Ḥayyim's profound knowledge of the Kabbalah, his dissociation of Halakhah from Kabbalah (except in an ultimate sense) is in practice so complete that from studying his Halakhah one would imagine he knew no Kabbalah at all.[85] No Kabbalah was taught in the Yeshivah of Volozhin.[86] Furthermore, as was mentioned earlier in this chapter, R. Ḥayyim sought to apply the Dissociation Principle even to pious sentiments within the range of normality: "fear," or what has been termed the devotional mood. This view certainly goes beyond the Gaon's concern for maintaining the separateness of Halakhah from charismatic experiences.

The third area of R. Ḥayyim's general concern with the tension and equilibrium between scholarship and piety, or *Torah* and *Yirah*, is his treatment of the devotional literature, the "books of *Yirah,*" or "books of *Musar.*" By and large, he reveals a moderately negative attitude toward this genre of pietistic writings, no doubt because he feared that the intellectually less taxing exercise might displace to too great an extent the more difficult, more demanding, and more valuable halakhic studies. R. Ḥayyim locates the origin of the popular didactic literature in an attempt to correct an earlier imbalance in favor of study of Torah:

> The earlier generations spent all their days in the study of and meditation in the holy Torah...and the flame of the love of the holy Torah burned in their hearts like a burning flame...until it came to pass that some of the students set aside all their time for and studied only the *pilpul* of Torah alone, and nothing else at all; whereas we learned in our Mishnah that if there is no *Yirah* there is no wisdom.[87]... Therefore a number of their great people, "the eyes of the community," those whose holy duty it was to concern themselves with the general weal of our brethren the House of Israel, bestirred themselves...to remove the obstacle from the path of the people of the Lord...and composed books of piety (*Yirah*) to set aright the heart of the people, that they might engage in the holy Torah and in worship in pure fear of the Lord.[88]

As a result, however, R. Ḥayyim finds that the pendulum has swung to the other extreme: preoccupation with the devotional works almost to the complete exclusion of proper study of Torah, that is, Halakhah, based on the erroneous assumption that the whole purpose of man in the world is to engage in the study of such devotional works because they inspire man to develop good traits; meanwhile, Torah itself is neglected.[89] R. Ḥayyim offers eyewitness testimony to the popularity of this pietistic literature and the consequent attrition of true scholarship:

> With my own eyes I saw in one district, where this [habit] became so widespread, that in most of their *Batei Midrash* there were many books of *Musar*, but nothing else, not even a complete set of the Talmud.⁹⁰

R. Ḥayyim naturally felt scandalized by this inversion of true values. If scholarship and piety are symbolized, respectively, by grain and storage house, the similes used by the Talmud, then the misguided, exclusive concentration on devotional literature is tantamount to spending one's life building storage houses without ever finally bringing the grain into it.

> So, how can one imagine that this is the purpose of a Jew, that he spend all his time set aside for study only in building the storage house of the fear of Heaven, when it is but an empty storehouse, and from all his toil he emerges with nothing more than the one commandment, "The Lord thy God shalt thou fear"?⁹¹

Even that one achievement remains in doubt: "It does not even earn the name of 'storage house' at all,"⁹² since it stores nothing within it. The whole genre of literature is, in essence, superfluous, for the study of Torah (i.e., Halakhah) *lishmah* itself inspires the piety that one must otherwise attempt to acquire artificially by means of perusing books of *Musar*.⁹³ Bothering with such work is a waste of precious time needed for study of Torah and is but the result of the nefarious subtlety of the evil urge.⁹⁴ Even when engaging in devotional studies, R. Ḥayyim recommends the study of appropriate classical rabbinic texts, such as Midrash or *Ein Ya'akov*, the collection of Aggadah, for these not only engender the devotional mood, but they are themselves texts of Torah, unlike the special devotional literature; such texts are therefore preferable to the standard books of *Musar*, "for then one does not involve himself in wasting time from Torah, Heaven forbid."⁹⁵ The only time that a scholar should betake himself to meditation in the *Musar* literature is when he is disturbed by special temptations; then he may search in it for the solution to his particular problem.[96] The devotional works thus have for R. Ḥayyim a limited validity; they are to be prescribed like medicine, not imbibed as part of one's general diet.

Further, R. Ḥayyim makes the point that the entire literature is beneath true scholars and should be reserved generally for the laity. Most important, he defines the *purpose* of devotional studies in a manner radically different from that advocated by the leaders of the *Musar* movement two generations later: "How exceedingly good and beautiful it is for laymen, who are always occupied in business, to study books of *Musar*, to arouse their dull hearts to set aside regular times for the study of Torah, including Halakhah and Aggadah, etc."[97] The function of the devotional period of study is, therefore, not the improvement of character as such, but the inspiration to study Torah with greater regularity and intensity.[98] Torah therefore remains supreme, and the devotional study is self-annihilating: its success is signified by the cessation of such study in favor of the study of Torah. In a later Hasidic polemical work, this theory is attributed to the Gaon. It is related that when the Gaon was once asked to speak words of *Musar*, his wry response was that you spank a child only to convince him to go to school and study; once he does so, there is no longer any need for striking him. So, the purpose of the devotional meditation is to urge the study of Torah; once a man studies, the devotional works are superfluous for him.[99]

R. Ḥayyim is not single-minded in his displeasure with what he considered the new fad of *Musar* literature. Thus, as was mentioned earlier, he counseled a brief period of devotional meditation before commencing to study, and he probably had in mind meditation that arises from reading this sort of writing. He considered all extant *Musar* works as good but recommended *Mesillat Yesharim* above all others.[100] But there can be little doubt that his strictures on the devotional mood apply equally for the devotional literature; the "books of *Yirah*" were, after all, composed for the purpose of inspiring *Yirah*. Hence for R. Ḥayyim any more than a minimal concern with books of *Musar* represents an unwarranted distraction from the pursuit of scholarship, which of itself inspires the same *Yirah* within the heart of the student. Thus on the Mishnah that relates that R. Joḥanan b. Zakkai instructed his students, "Go out and see which is the good way to which a man should cling,"[101] R. Ḥayyim comments:

> He hinted to them by the word "go out" that when you are *within* the study hall do not ponder the problems of character traits and the right ways of conduct [i.e., the substance of the *Musar* works], for this is the seduction of the Evil Urge to take you away from Torah, and afterwards lead you on to other things; therefore he said, "*go out* and see," that only after you leave the study hall is it the proper time to ponder the question of which is the good way, etc.[102]

On the basis of the above, exception must be taken to the efforts of some of the leading figures of the *Musar* movement in the nineteenth century, followed by some contemporary historians of the movement, to identify R. Ḥayyim as one of the forefathers of *Musar*. The search for distinguished antecedents is an expected and respected part of any new impulse and changing perspective within the Jewish tradition. Thus the tendency in *Musar* circles was to trace the origin of their movement, founded by R. Israel Lipkin of Salant (Salanter),[103] through his teacher R. Zondel, to his teacher, R. Ḥayyim, and through R. Ḥayyim, in turn, to his teacher, the Gaon of Vilna.[104] Here the line stops, probably because of a combination of the overwhelming authority of the Gaon, and because he was both far enough from them in time and yet not too far; going back into earlier history would have blurred the origins of *Musar* as an organized movement. Even then, the evidence for the theory of the Gaon as the founder or even a precursor of the ethicist movement is meager indeed. Dov Katz briefly points to the fact that the Gaon recommended meditation in devotional works.[105] But all this proves is that he found this kind of literature acceptable and morally edifying. However, this hardly makes of the Gaon a "Musarite," for in a life of creative and copious writing, and with no evidence of any clear opposition to such devotional studies, such stray remarks are totally inadequate to identify him as the originator or architect of the *Musar* movement, still three generations away.

When they come to R. Hayyim and place him in the line of succession, we find even more juggling of the facts. The search for antecedents is most prominent in the writings of R. Isaac Blazer ("Reb Itzelle Peterburger"), one of the three most distinguished disciples of R. Israel [Lipkin] Salanter. Blazer quotes that portion of *Nefesh ha-Hayyim* that permits a brief period of meditation in the middle of one's studies[106] – which, it will be recalled, is clearly a concession on the part of R. Hayyim – and then attaches to it a statement from another chapter in which R. Hayyim clearly intends to minimize the time spent on devotional meditation without necessarily fixing the length of time in advance; but to Blazer, it becomes something quite different, an escape clause. R. Hayyim writes:

> For it was not permitted to engage in the contemplation and acquisition of *Yirah*, except as one can estimate intelligently that, in accordance with his own nature and condition, this is the amount of time that is needed and necessary for him to engage in the acquisition of *Yirah* and *Musar*.[107]

Blazer interprets this in a manner that opens the door to the study of *Musar* for any length of time, depending upon one's own subjective judgment: "And from this one can estimate how much time is necessary for him to take account of himself before his Owner in purity of heart and fear of the Lord."[108] All the intervening material from *Nefesh ha-Hayyim* – R. Hayyim's limitations, his assessment of the approximate length of time to be spent on meditation, his evaluation of scholarship as always superior to devotion – is omitted from Blazer's eclectic quotation. His conclusion is, therefore, that "without doubt he [R. Zondel] received his method of *Musar* study from his teacher, R. Ḥayyim of Volozhin."[109] Dov Katz, the foremost historian of *Musar*, accepts uncritically Blazer's spiritual genealogy. He is sure that R. Ḥayyim was a precursor of *Musar* because of his "sharp criticism" of theearlier generations who devoted all their time to *pilpul* and none to *Musar*;[110] actually, an objective reading of the passage in *Nefesh ha-Ḥayyim* yields no such impression. R. Ḥayyim is merely explaining why earlier generations did not meditate in *Yirah* – because they were preoccupied by study; and why later it became necessary to institute such periods of meditation and study of didactical literature – for the Evil Urge tempted them to the sole and exclusive preoccupation with halakhic studies, thereby violating the Mishnah's admonition against the pursuit of "wisdom" without "fear."[111] Compared with his brooding denunciation, both before and after this passage in the same chapter, of those who swayed to the other extreme, this historical theory of the emergence of a popular devotional literature is not "sharp" or "scathing" by any standards. Katz recognizes that R. Ḥayyim had very serious reservations about the entire literature and the exaggerated importance already being placed upon it, but then proceeds to dismiss it as trivial or irrelevant to the main brunt of R. Ḥayyim's outlook, which "without doubt... conforms to that of the Gaon, who was so infinitely great and holy in his eyes" in approving the study of *Musar* as it was later programmed by R. Israel Salanter and his disciples.[112] Katz further tries to bolster his point by showing that R. Ḥayyim's personal life revealed qualities later expounded and expanded upon by *Musar*, such as modesty, service, and love of fellow man.[113] However, the fact that a man is ethical does not precommit him to a specific ethical philosophy; R. Ḥayyim's character may have been exemplary, as it most certainly was according to all the evidence we have, but it is unwarranted to deduce therefrom that he subscribed to the Musarite evaluation of devotional study vis-à-vis halakhic study.

R. Isaac Blazer himself, for all his efforts at locating a spiritual precursor in R. Ḥayyim, recognized that the movement of which he was a leading light did not follow the pattern recommended by R. Ḥayyim:

> R. Ḥayyim of Volozhin, may the memory of the righteous be a blessing, once said that the Evil Urge approaches man indirectly and says: "Speak about me as much as you want, provided that meanwhile you waste time from the study of Torah." To this R. Isaac Peterburger [Blazer], of blessed memory, added: That was in those days; today, however, the Evil Urge says, "study, study, provided you don't talk about me."[114]

Allowing for epigrammatic license in a *bon mot*, this passage does indicate the new and changing directions taken by the developing *Musar* movement. Indeed, upon the death of R. Israel Salanter, his student, the same R. Isaac Blazer, introduced *Musar* studies on par with talmudic studies, to the distress and chagrin of much of the rabbinic world.[115] This is certainly, from R. Ḥayyim's point of view, a disproportionate amount of time.

R. Ḥayyim's Dissociation Principle, his methodological dualism that kept the provinces of scholarship and piety strictly separate, was thus consistently followed by him, at least in theory, for the entire catalogue of items that might be included in the generic term of devotion, or *Yirah*, fear, as opposed to halakhic study. Halakhic scholarship must be distinct from charismatic experiences, as the Gaon had taught; from the study of Kabbalah, even diverging from the Gaon's policy; from the devotional experience of *devekut* and the devotional mood or "fear of sin," contrary to Hasidic doctrine; and from the study of and meditation in devotional literature, contrary to what others – whether Hasidim or, later, the Musarites – taught. The two realms were separate and unequal. The supremacy of Torah remained unimpeachable.[116]

Notes

1. *Pe'ah* 1:1, and elsewhere throughout the entire literature. See end of chap. VII in this book.
2. *Nefesh ha-Ḥayyim* (hereinafter: *NH*) 4:10.
3. *Sifrei* (ed. M. Friedmann), *Ekev*, 48; *Avot* 6:1; *Nedarim* 62a, etc.
4. The documentation for this assertion, as well as the previously mentioned Torah concept of R. Ḥayyim and his definition of *Torah lishmah*, is too extensive for the purposes of this essay. A more elaborate discussion and appropriate references may be found in my *Torah Lishmah: Torah for Torah's Sake in the Works of Rabbi Ḥayyim of Volozhin and His Contemporaries* (Hoboken, N.J.: Ktav, 1989), chaps. III–VIII. See also my "Pukhovitzer's Concept of *Torah Lishmah*," in *Jewish Social Studies*, vol. XXX, no. 3 July 1968.
5. *Sifrei, loc. cit.; Berakhot* 17a; J.T. *Berakhot* 1:5; *Sefer Hasidim*, ed. R. Margaliot (Jerusalem: Mosad Harav Kook, 1950), no. 944; R.E. de Vidas, *Reshit Hokhmah* (Jerusalem and New York, 1937), Introduction, pp. 2a, 3b; R.I. ha-L. Horowitz, *Shenei Luḥot ha-Berit* (Jerusalem, חמו"ל, 1969), pp. 99–101.
6. *Berakhot* 5b; *Midrash Tehillim* (ed. S. Buber) 31:9, pp. 240 f.; all through *Seder Eliyahu*, see Introduction by Friedman to his edition of this work, pp. 109–113.
7. *Sifrei* (ed. M. Friedmann (Ish Shalom)), *Va-etḥanan*, 32, p. 73a; *Sotah* 31a; J.T. *Berakhot* 9:7 and *Sotah* 5:5; Maimonides, Commentary to the Mishnah, end of *Makkot*, and Code, *Hilkhot Teshuvah*, 10:4, 5; *Sefer Hasidim*, no. 289; Naḥmanides, Commentary to the Pentateuch, to Deut. 6:5; Crescas, *Or Adonai*, 2:6, chaps. i and ii.
8. *Zohar Hadash, Tikkunim*, pp. 63a, b; R.H. Vital, *Peri Etz Ḥayyim*, beginning of *Sha'ar Hanhagat ha-Limmud*.
9. *Keter Shem Tov*, p. 19c; R. Phinḥas of Korets, *Likkutim Yekarim*, p. 4b; R. Jacob Joseph of Polonne, *Toledot Ya'akov Yosef* (Lvov, Defus Yisrael Elimelech Stand, 1863) to *Va-yetzei*, p. 28d, and to *Shelaḥ*, p. 123d; R. Yosef Yitzḥak of Lubavitch, *Likkutei Dibburim*, vol. III, no. 22, pp. 890–892; cf. G. Scholem, "Devekuth, or Communion with God," *Review of Religion*, vol. XIV, no. 2 (January 1950), 125.
10. *NH* 4:3, based on *Nedarim* 62a, and commentary of R. Asher, thereon; cf. *Avot de-Rabbi Nathan* (Version A) to *Avot* 2:12.
11. Thus, *Sifrei* (ed. M. Friedmann (Ish Shalom)), *Ekev*, 48, *Berakhot* 17a *et al.*
12. Thus, *inter al., NH* 1:21, pre-4:2 ("pre-4" refers to the unnumbered section between parts 3 and 4), 4:7.

13. The term refers specifically to study as distinct from prayer, for the Dissociation Principle (on which see below) was meant especially for the former as distinguished from the latter. Thus, the Mitnagged in *Mezaref Avodah*, a pseudepigraphic pro-Hasidic polemic, is at one point willing to grant to his Hasidic controversialist the need for fervor and religious zeal in prayer, which he had previously denied, but withholds such acquiescence from the Hasidic requirement of devotional consciousness and enthusiasm during the course of study of Torah, because of the incompatibility of devotional meditation and ratiocination: ...כי בתפילה יכול להיות שדרכיכם ישר שצריך להיות בהתלהבות ובהתבוננות, אבל בלימוד התורה לפי דעתנו זהו דבר שא״א כי זמן תורה לחוד וזמן תפילה לחוד מצרף עבודה (p. 45.). See n. 36 below.

14. This term should be taken in its generic sense of piety, and not as fear in contradistinction to love as a specific religious emotion. Thus the term as employed by R. Ḥayyim would no doubt include the love of God, which, according to some, such as Maimonides (n. 7 above), is the essence of *lishmah*. If by "love" is meant the contemplative love intended, e.g., by Maimonides, this will be covered in the second of the three categories, that of the devotional *mood*; if it is taken to mean the affective, emotional, ecstatic love, as the Hasidim generally interpreted it, it belongs to the first of these categories, the devotional *experience*.

15. See esp. *NH* 4:2. For some aspects of R. Ḥayyim's critique, see chap. VI of this book.

16. In addition to R. Ḥayyim's personal discipline and almost Spartan restraint mentioned by his biographer (Mosheh Shmuel Shapiro-Shmukler, "תולדות רבנו חיים מוואלוז׳ין" [Bene-Berak, 1957]), his displeasure with any untoward and immodest display of emotion is illustrated by the incident of "Rabbi Berach the Galician," a highly emotional itinerant preacher who attracted large audiences to his sermons. R. Ḥayyim, despite the hesitations of many leading rabbis, was skeptical of the preacher's hysterics and histrionics and pursued him until he was forcibly ejected from a synagogue in Minsk, in about 1810. R. Ḥayyim's antagonism to Rabbi Berach was based upon a letter, now lost to us, to R. Ḥayyim from R. Ephraim Zalman Margolies. We do not know exactly what happened to this preacher; it is conjectured that he either became an apostate or went mad. (Y. Lifschitz, "זכרון יעקב" [Kovno-Slobodka, 1924] I, pp. 24 f., and cf. his article in "הכרם," 1898; and Shapiro-Shmukler, pp. 144–148. These sources also tell of R. Ḥayyim's highly developed intuition in suspecting "The Crimean," a Czarist police spy looking for Jews dealing in contraband; R. Ḥayyim's actions saved Vilna Jewry.)

17. A. Kariv, "ליטא מכורתי" in "יהדות ליטא" (Jerusalem: Mosad Harav Kook, 1959), pp. 9f. Lithuanian Jews, Kariv writes, even observed the commandment "Thou shalt be joyous in thy festivals" with solemnity. The only time they permitted themselves to drink beer near the synagogue was on שמחת תורה, and its total effect was to make them sing "ברוך אלקינו". This was the only time, other than a wedding or other שמחה של מצוה, that there was any community singing of a happy nature.

18. Thus the story of the "dreamer" reported by R. Ḥayyim toward the end of his Foreword to the "באור הגר״א על ספרא דצניעותא". (R. Ḥayyim relates that he heard this directly from the Gaon himself.) A Vilna Jew who was reputed to have revealed secret knowledge gained by means of dreams was brought before the Gaon. He told the Gaon that two weeks earlier he had heard certain discourses in Torah while R. Simeon b. Yoḥai sat on his right and R. Isaac Luria on his left. The Gaon paled when he heard the story – he evidently regarded the dream as substantially true and a case of valid clairvoyance; he looked deeply into the dreamer's face and recognized that he was probably a melancholiac who, despite his psychological aberrations, often experienced true dreams. He therefore commanded that the dreamer be banished.

19. The ideal halakhic personality, according to Rabbi Joseph B. Soloveitchik ("איש ההלכה," in *Talpiyyot* [1944], 1:3–4, p. 699), is wary of becoming intoxicated with joy, without any basis for its magnitude in logic or reason, preferring instead what William James has called "solemnity," an affective life that keeps to moderation and away from the extremes of excessive joy or despair. This emotional quietude, which stoic quality befits the esteem of the halakhist for the intellect, was particularly characteristic of R. Ḥayyim. His opposition to the exaggerated experientialism of the Hasidim is thus not only a matter of taste and personal predisposition, but a reflection of R. Ḥayyim's successful achievement of the ideal halakhic personality, the "איש ההלכה" described by Rabbi Soloveitchik. This does not mean, of course, the abandonment of all emotion or experience in favor of the implementation of an objective, legalistic, *a priori*, and impersonal "system," which would reduce the religious life of the Jew to an intellectualized, ritualistic behaviorism. The concern of R. Ḥayyim for *Yirah* and his intense preoccupation with Kabbalah certainly belie any such notions. R. Ḥayyim does, however, follow the ideal typology later adumbrated by Rabbi Soloveitchik in that his religious experiences are more inward than outward, more intensive and contemplative than ecstatic, as befits one who holds that experience follows and must be based upon cognition (*ibid.*, p. 704).

20. Thus R. Pinḥas of Korets, "ליקוטים יקרים" (Chernowitz, 1864), p. 2c.

21. *NH* 4:4.
22. *Yoma* 72b.
23. *NH* 4:4.
24. *Shabbat* 31a.
25. *NH* 4:4.
26. *NH* 4:5.
27. *Ibid.*
28. One could hardly be more mistaken than S.Y. Charna ("רבי חיים" מוולוז'ין בתור פדגוג" in "שבילי החינוך" of 'חשון תרפ"ט, שנה ד' חוברת ו) p. 312, who, describing R. Ḥayyim's negative reaction to the extreme pietism of Hasidism, maintains that הוא רוצה בסינתיזה של הלמוד עם היראה, בסינתיזה המביאה לידי חכמה. R. Ḥayyim, in fact, wants not a synthesis in which each element loses its identity, but an accommodation or coexistence of the two in the context of one personality.
29. *NH* pre-4:2, and 4:1. See n. 15 above and n. 36 below.
30. Nn. 25–27 above.
31. N. 24 above.
32. 4:9. R. Ḥayyim's mention of "robbery" refers to *Shabbat* 31a, where Rava compares the relation of *Yirah* to *Torah* with that of preservative to produce; without at least a *kav* of the former, a whole *kur* of the latter is spoiled. The Talmud (*ibid.*) then appends a remark relating this metaphor to a literal case in financial law: a man who sells a *kur* of grain may include in it a *kav* of the preservative without fear of violating the law of deceit, that is, stealing from the buyer the amount by which a *kav* of grain costs more than a *kav* of preservative. What R. Ḥayyim means, therefore, is that only a *kav* of preservative is permitted; more than that constitutes fraud or misrepresentation. Hence, in terms of the metaphor, the amount of time allotted to *Yirah* over and above the amount needed for the preservation of *Torah* constitutes theft or fraud (See n. 40 below.)
33. *NH, loc. cit.*
34. *NH* 4:10. What R. Ḥayyim says here of *devekut* applies *a fortiori* to יראת חטא, for if study of Torah automatically constitutes the former, which is usually defined (i.e., by Hasidism) as an active and intense experience, certainly so is it an act of the latter, a far more passive state of mind.
35. Thus for R. Joseph Karo, דבקות and הרהורא דאורייתא are identical. Throughout his "מגיד מישרים," *devekut* means meditating on Halakhah in general and, for Karo, on Mishnah in particular. "Karo's *Maggid* expresses the typically rabbinic view of the matter: the study of the

law can simply be equated with *devekut*. The *Torah* is God's word, His revealed logos, a mystical manifestation of the Shekhinah," R.J.Z. Werblowsky, *Joseph Karo: Lawyer and Mystic* (London: Oxford University Press, 1962), p. 158.

36. *NH* 4:3. This Hasidic rebuttal to the *NH*, the pseudepigraphic *Mezaref Avodah*, mentioned earlier, appreciates the fact that R. Ḥayyim restricts the Dissociation Principle only to study but not to practice (including prayer). Thus on p. 45: אם ילמוד בכל עת לימודו בה בהתלהבות כדרכיכם ימעט מלימודו מחמת התבוננות בענין היראה ויגזול את לימודו. At the same time: בתפילה יכול להיות שדרכיכם ישר שצריך להיות בהתלהבות ובהתבוננות, אבל בלימוד התורה לפי דעתנו זהו דבר שא״א... See n. 13 above.

37. Note the distinction between *devekut* and "fear of the Lord" and "fear of sin." The former, when consciously observed, is an intense, galvanizing experience; but when one studies the Torah, according to R. Ḥayyim, one enacts *devekut* even in the absence of this emotional experience. "Fear," however, is the setting of the devotional *mood* rather than *experience* and hence is recommended by R. Ḥayyim even when *devekut* is observed automatically by means of study of Torah. See next note.

38. *NH* 4:6. R. Ḥayyim thus identifies Halakhah as the Will and Aggadah as the Word of God; but since the two are identical with the divine essence, therefore the study of any part of Torah is an act of *devekut* with God. It must be emphasized that when R. Ḥayyim declares study to be an automatic *devekut*, he accepts – as he does whenever using the term – the Hasidic version of the concept. This, however, is *not* the meaning of *lishmah*, for *lishmah*, unlike *devekut*, requires much greater discrimination; because of its primary intellectualistic sense, it applies with much greater force to Halakhah than to Scripture or, presumably, Aggadah. Thus his criticism of the Hasidic interpretation of *lishmah* as *devekut* in *NH* 4:2.

39. R. Ḥayyim's literalness in this case may be more than a fortuitous instance of a text that he could not help but interpret in a clever homiletic fashion to prove his point. His student R. Zondel Salanter recalls in his name that the Talmud's principle that אין מקרא יוצא מדי פשוטו refers not only to Scripture but also to the words of the Sages, that is, Talmud, and the Kabbalah(!) as well. It is also reported that one Friday afternoon, after the students had left the Yeshivah in Volozhin in order to prepare for the Sabbath, R. Ḥayyim was found rolling on the floor of the Bet ha-Midrash. He explained that he was executing literally the words of the Mishnah (*Avot* 1:4), והוי מתאבק בעפר רגליהם, that one must "roll in the

dust of the feet" of scholars of Torah: figuratively, one must pay close attention to their teachings (D. Katz, "תנועת המוסר" [Tel Aviv, 1950], vol. I, p. 108, n. 12). The story is probably apocryphal and does not have much verisimilitude in the light of what we know of R. Ḥayyim's general personal restraint and sobriety. It is, nevertheless, an interesting insight into his reputed tendency to take the words of the Talmud literally.

40. See n. 32 above. The Talmud recommends a maximum of a *kav* of preservative to a *kur* of produce. R. Ḥayyim calculates this, based on talmudic weights and measures, to be in the proportion of 1:180, hence, programmatically, five minutes to fifteen hours. The Hasidic rebuttal manages to interpret the same text to arrive at a much greater allowance for *Yirah*: one quarter-hour at the beginning, followed by one hour of study; then if all is "going well," only about two minutes are needed for the next hour, and so on. (*Mezaref Avodah*, p. 48.) n. 58 below.

41. *Avot* 3:9: רבי חנינא בן דוסא אומר כל שיראת חטאו קודמת לחכמתו חכמתו מתקימת. R. Ḥayyim takes it in its chronological sense as priority in time, rather than as a value judgment, priority in importance.

42. *Ruaḥ Ḥayyim* (on 1:1), p. 10.

43. *NH* 4:7. R. Ḥayyim justifies this midday meditation by referring again to the talmudic metaphor: the preservative, too, must be well distributed throughout the produce if it is to be effective. See n. 58 below.

44. Cf. *NH* 4:2.

45. *NH* 4:7: ולזאת ראוי להאדם להכין עצמו כל עת קודם שיתחיל ללמוד. להתחשב מעט עם קונו. ית"ש בטהרת הלב בידאת ה׳ As it appears literally, it would seem that "יראת ה׳" is itself a distinct unit, the first of four. However, this is in all probability a stylistic awkwardness and is intended as the generalization, with the specifics – three of them – to follow.

46. *Ibid*.

47. *Ibid*.: כדי שיוכל להתקשר ולהתדבק בעת עסקו בתוה"ק בדבורו ורצונו ית"ש. Alternatively, these first two may be read as one: to repent from sin in order better to be able to achieve this *devekut* through Torah. R. Ḥayyim's style is imprecise and thus results in this ambiguity, but the sense of the passage would indicate the three separate elements mentioned.

48. *Ibid*. This recalls the prayer composed by R. Isaiah ha-Levi Horowitz for recital prior to the study of Torah: "שני לוחות הברית" (Jerusalem, 1959), מסכת שבועות, pp. 99–191.

49. Both R. Ḥayyim and R. Shneour Zalman resort to the idea of changed circumstances, usually for the worse, in order to reconcile their views with conflicting texts. Thus R. Shneour Zalman considers the contemporary elevation of worship over study a result of the

debilitation of the spirit since tannaitic days (see his שער קריאת שמע in "סידור הלב"; his letter, cited by H.M. Heilman, "בית רבי" (Berdichev: Y. Dazumovsky, 1903), pp. 38f; and "ליקוטי תורה" to ואתחנן p. 12b). R. Ḥayyim, similarly, concedes the need for a devotional literature because the worsening spiritual condition of the times requires it (*NH* 4:1.). Yet R. Ḥayyim prefaces this statement by remarking that in his immediate age the spirit is in an especially low estate, to wit, the tendency to replace halakhic studies with devotional works (*ibid.*). See also the reference, to R. Pinḥas of Korets in n. 20 above.

50. "הנהגות ישרות" (מוסר ומדות מהבעש"ט הקדוש זצ"ל, מודא מקדש על קדושת. p. 11a. בית הכנסת להרה"ק מהר"ר יעקב יוסף מפולנאה, לשצוב, תקע"ו)

51. In "צוואת הריב"ש".

52. *Sukkah* 28a.

53. The Besht interprets מרכבה not as the name of a doctrine or study, but literally as a vehicle, in keeping with the kabbalistic idea that each man, like the Patriarchs, must become a "vehicle" for God by submerging his will and ego entirely in offering to become His spokesman or means of carrying out the divine will and purpose in the world.

54. "כתר שם טוב", p. 16b.

55. "ליקוטים יקרים", p. 4d. This is already recommended by the Talmud (J.T. *Shekalim* 2:5, end), but without the explanation of its effectiveness.

56. "צוואת הריב"ש".

57. "כתר שם טוב" 11, p. 22b: המהלך (אבות פרק ג') במשנה ז"ל חכמינו שאמרו ענין וזהו בדרך ושונה ומפסיק ממשנתו...ויש לומר דהפירוש הוא שהולך בדרך הישר ואפילו הכי יחידי, שאינו דבוק בהשם יתברך, ושונה ומפסיק ממשנתו ר"ל מפסיק עצמו מהשם יתברך מחמת משנתו.

58. N. 40 above. However, R. Ḥayyim too "permits" a very brief period of meditation in the middle, and not only at the beginning, of one's studies; see *NH* 4:7 (n. 43 above). Although the difference practically may seem to be merely a question of the economy of time in the construction of a curriculum, the essential theories that inform the different points of view are of paramount significance in defining both the purpose of Torah and its position in the hierarchy of Judaism's values. Furthermore, *Mezaref Avodah* is a relatively late Hasidic work and, despite its polemical nature, shows a decided inclination toward reconciliation, and has thus already benefited from R. Ḥayyim's objections to original Hasidic doctrine (see my article on the *Mezaref Avodah* in the *Joshua Finkel Festschrift* published by Yeshiva University in 1974). Further, R. Ḥayyim's acquiescence to a period of devotional meditation in the middle of the course of study is clearly a concession that is offered by R. Ḥayyim only begrudgingly; see later in this chapter.

59. "מצרף עבודה", p. 48.

60. See the beginning of this chapter and nn. 16–19.

61. Werblowsky, *Joseph Karo*, pp. 307f.

62. R. Ḥayyim (in his Introduction to Gaon's "שנות אליהו," a commentary on Mishnah *Seder Zeraim*) refers to many unpublished manuscripts by the Gaon on Kabbalah. Rabbi Joseph B. Soloveitchik relates that he met one of the last survivors of the old preachers (מטיפים) of the *Hovevei Zion* movement, R. Yehudah Leib Yevzerov (d. Bayit va-Gan near Tel Aviv, in 1935), who told him of having visited R. Shemaryahu Zuckerman in Mohilev, on the Dnieper, who took him to his attic and there showed him an iron storage box full of unpublished manuscripts of the Gaon on Kabbalah (J.I. Dienstag, "רבנו אליהו מווילנא; רשימה ביבליוגרפית" in "תלפיות" [July 1949], p. 269, n. 6).

63. R. Ḥayyim's *Foreword* to the "באור הגר״א על ספרא דצניעותא".

64. Ibid.

65. Werblowsky, *Joseph Karo*, p. 22.

66. R. Ḥayyim's *Foreword*. Whereas this particular reference is to esoteric knowledge, it is apparent from other passages taken in context, such as his reference to the *Maggid* of R. Joseph Karo, that he includes halakhic information as well. Indeed, revelations of halakhic content have a rather long history; see, e.g., E.E. Urbach's "בעלי התוספות" (1955), pp. 154, 174–175, and the Introduction by R.R. Margoliot to his edition (Jerusalem: Mosad Harav Kook, 1957) of the twelfth-century "תשובות מן השמים" by R. Jacob the Pious of Marvege. Werblowsky, *Joseph Karo* (p. 15 f) has shown that *Maggidim* and other such paranormal phenomena were far more widespread and valued by well-known writers than hitherto realized. Perhaps one reason may be the traditional reluctance of Jewish mystics to speak of their intimate experiences, thus exercising a kind of self-censorship; see G. Scholem, *Major Trends in Jewish Mysticism*, pp. 15, 16, 147.

67. R. Ḥayyim's *Foreword*: והההשגות ע״י המלאכים המגידים ושרי התורה אשר לא עמלתי ולא חכמתי אין לי בהם חפץ.

68. R.H. Vital, "ספר הגלגולים" (Przemysl, 1876), p. 87b; "לקוטים," end שער הגלגולים. Vital maintains that Karo was occasionally misled by his *Maggid*. The Gaon, however, apparently did not question the authenticity of Karo's *Maggid*'s teachings but did suspect such phenomena in his own times:

ואמר אף כי מרן הב״י הי׳ לו מגיד, היה זה לפני ב׳ מאות שנה שהיו הדורות כתיקונן, והי׳ שרוי על אדמת הקודש, לא כן עתה שרבו המתפרצים ובפרט בחו״ל א״א כלל שיהיה כולו קדש קדשים בלי שום עירוב כלל, ובפרט הגלויים אשר לא בתורה נפשו בחלה בהם ולא היו נחשבים אצלו

כלל וכלל (R. Ḥayyim's *Foreword*). It is not unlikely that by the epithet המתפרצים, the Gaon was referring to the Hasidim, and especially to the Besht, who also reported extended עליות נשמה and considerable revelations. See n. 71 below.

69. N. 67 above.

70. R. Ḥayyim's *Foreword*: ששלח רבינו אותי אצל אחי הקטן והגדול ממני בכל מילי דמטיב חסידא קדישא הגאון מוהר"ש זלמן זללה"ה לאמר לו בצווי משמו שלא יקבל שום מלאך מגיד אשר יבא אצלו, כי בזמן לא כביר יבא אליו מלאך מגיד.

Interestingly, a remarkably similar story is related elsewhere in a manner that emphasizes the difference between this approach and that of the Hasidim. A grandson of R. Yizḥak Shor of Gwazdicz relates the following, told to him by the eminent halakhic scholar R. Joseph Shaul Nathanson, Rabbi of Lvov, in 1873, which he, in turn, heard from those who knew R. Yizḥak Shor personally. The latter had several chance meetings with R. Israel Besht, and the Besht was deeply impressed by both his scholarship and piety. At the third of these meetings, the Besht said to him, "The prophet Elijah sent me to inform you that tonight he will appear to you." The answer of R. Yizḥak Shor – even more emphatic than that of the Gaon in R. Ḥayyim's report – was: "I desire neither him [Elijah] nor you. I study Torah *lishmah* and Heaven forfend that I be distracted even for a brief moment from my studies" (Introduction to R. Yizḥak Shor, "שו"ת כח שור" [Kolome, A. Teicher, 1888]). A similar story attributing to Hasidim this aversion to Torah gained without intellectual effort is told by Rabbi S.Y. Zevin ("ספורי חסידים" to בחוקותי, no. 301) concerning R. Aaron Leib of Premishlan and R. Elimelekh of Lizensk. However, the story is unreliable and is quoted in an entirely different fashion in other sources; see Bezalel Landau, "הרבי ר' אלימלך מליזענסק" (Jerusalem, Or haChasidut, 1963), pp. 126 f., and p. 190, n. 22.

71. R.A. Cohen, "מאמרים ומעשיות שונות" end "כתר ראש - אורחות חיים," no. 2. This is in keeping with the ambivalent attitude of R. Ḥayyim toward the Gaon's mystical adventures as expressed in his *Foreword*. There he both admires the Gaon's charismatic prowess and yet approvingly cites the Gaon's own distrust of the resultant revelations. Interestingly, the same source (*ibid.*, no. 13) cites the Gaon (apparently quoted by R. Ḥayyim) as attributing nocturnal mystical dream experiences to the Besht! גילו להגר"א זל"ה בחלום כמה סודות בשם מ"ב...ואמר כל מה שהבעש"ט ידע היה ע"י שאלת חלום בכל לילה. At first blush, this is nothing less than fantastic, especially in the light of R. Shneour Zalman's complaint that the Gaon and the Mitnaggedim refuse to acknowledge that the Hasidic doctrines originate in revelations by Elijah (Heilman, p. 40–43). Nevertheless,

this may possibly be genuine and reflect that Gaon's contempt for easy and effortless pneumatic triumphs. This possibility is confirmed by his conversation with R. Ḥayyim, in which he grants the possibility, but not the full authenticity, of contemporary mystical revelations, and especially his reference to המתפרצים, n. 68 above. It should be pointed out that this book was published in 1819, while R. Ḥayyim was still alive, and publication of the Gaon's comment about the Besht must have been seen and, to judge from the absence of any recorded reaction to the contrary, approved by R. Ḥayyim. Cf. the articles on the Gaon by H.H. Ben Sasson, in *Zion* (1966), pp. 39–86, 197–216, and in my *Torah Lishmah*, chap. 1, pp. 41–45.

72. The term, coined by Werblowsky (*Joseph Karo*, p. 43), is stylistically felicitous but can be misleading. The Gaon was both a halakhist and a supernaturalist, as the above sources make abundantly clear, especially considering that the Gaon committed to writing many of the esoteric mysteries revealed to him supernaturally (n. 63 above). What the Gaon opposed was the free crossing of the boundaries between the two domains – in other words, what we have termed the "Dissociation Principle."

73. Werblowsky, *Joseph Karo*, p. 43.

74. See n. 67 above: אשר לו עמלתי ולא חכמתי. So too in passages referred to in nn. 66 and 71.

75. See "אמרי שפר" in "סידור הגר״א" on the Blessings of the Torah:
הידיעה היא גוף התורה ועיקרה, והעסק היא מצוה מתרי״ג מצוות...והידיעה, לידע את התורה מצוותיה ודרכיה, היא עיקר התורה, שעי״ז אנו דבקים בו ית׳ ומזדכך נפשינו ורוחינו.

This would indicate that the Gaon esteemed the possession of sacred knowledge more than the process of its acquisition, the reverse of R. Ḥayyim's judgment. Nevertheless, it is abundantly clear that the intellectual endeavor is a prerequisite and of great value in the opinion of the Gaon.

76. Werblowsky (*Joseph Karo*, p. 41, n. 2) correctly relates the emphasis on עמל and the rejection of indoctrination, by vision or inspiration, to the Talmudic conception of the ultimate bliss of the soul as the study of Torah in the celestial academy. This is contrasted by him with the usual definition of mysticism in Catholic doctrine, that of the anticipation of the blessed vision in this life.

77. *NH* 4:2.

78. From a manuscript copy by R.J. Zondel, in E. Rivlin, "הצדיק ר׳ יוסף זונדל ורבותיו" (Jerusalem: 1887), p. 111.

79. *Ibid.*, p. 110.

80. Cf. "עליות אליהו," p. 33. R. Boruch Epsztejn "מקור ברוך," vol. III, p. 1563 f., records an incident characteristic of the Gaon's phenomenal intensity in his intellectual endeavors, as related by R. Ḥayyim, who was an eyewitness, to the latter's nephew, R. Abraham Simḥah of Amstislow.
81. R. Israel of Shklov, "פאת השלחן," Introduction.
82. R. Ḥayyim, Foreword.
83. R. Ḥayyim, Open Letter, announcing the establishment of the Yeshivah of Volozhin; for the best version, see Samuel K. Mirsky, "ישיבת וולוזין" in his "מוסדות התורה באירופה בבנינם ובחורבנם" (New York: 'Ogen, 1956), p. 5.
84. Rav Zair (Chaim Tchernowitz), "תולדות הפוסקים," II, p. 278; J. Dienstag, in Talpiyyot, vol. IV (1949–1950), p. 263, n. 70.
85. Shapiro-Shmukler, תולדות p. 193. See, however, the story he cites from Frumkin about R. Elijah Kalischer's discovery of R. Ḥayyim's disguised Kabbalism in his halakhic exposition, ibid., p. 175 f, n. 4. See too B. Landau "הגאון החסיד מווילנא" (Jerusalem: Usha, 1965), p. 142, n. 20.
86. Charna, "רבי חיים," p. 314.
87. Avot 3:17.
88. NH 4:1. R. Ḥayyim probably had in mind the proto-Hasidic literature which prepared the way, psychologically, for the advent of Hasidism and which was then quite popular.
89. Ibid.
90. Ibid.
91. NH 4:8.
92. Ibid.
93. NH 4:9. R. Ḥayyim's emphasis on study of Torah lishmah as giving rise to piety is meant not to exclude she-lo lishmah as having such a beneficial side effect, but to exclude the devotional definitions that require a consciousness of some element other than the cognitive examination of the subject matter.
94. NH 4:9, and see nn. 102 and 114 below. This emphasis and the role assigned to the evil urge by R. Ḥayyim is paralleled by the diametrically opposite view of the Besht, who regards study of Gemara and its commentaries to the exclusion of the study of Musar as submission to the blandishments of the evil urge ("צוואת הריב״ש").
95. R. Asher Cohen, "כתר ראש - אורחות חיים," end תורה תלמוד הל׳.
96. Ibid. Cf. R. Ḥayyim of Brisk's rejection of the request by R. Isaac Blazer that Musar studies be instituted in Volozhin. R. Ḥayyim maintained that a normal, healthy organism does not need radical medicines – so, too, a healthy Jew studies Torah. Only if he is "sick" does he need anything as severe as the Musar studies. See Rabbi J.B. Soloveitchik, "איש ההלכה," loc. cit., p. 698.

97. *Ibid.* Cf. n. 102 below.

98. Most devotees of the study of *Musar*, even before the birth of the movement by that name, did not conceive of it as primarily a means of encouraging the study of Torah. R. Ḥayyim's attitude should be contrasted with for example that of R. Jonathan Eybeschütz (ca. 1690–1764), for whom the devotional introduction to Halakhah study is meant expressly to teach the student that practice, and not study, is most important: אהובי בני ואחיי כבר אמרתי לכם זה כמה פעמים כי לחדול הרע צריך הכנה קלה והיא טובה עד מאד כמו הרופאים שנותנים לאדם לאכול כל יום בתמידות בבקר וערב משקל איזה גרעין מסמים ומרקחת לחיך וזה טוב לו יותר משימתין עד שיחלה ואח״כ ישתה רפואות לרוב שהם כחרבות לגוף מבלבלים הטבע זכן מי שבשם ישראל יכונה החיוב עליו לקרות בכל יום ערב ובקר איזה דפין מספרי מוסר אשר הס ת״ל רבים בדפוס ומהקדוש לה׳ ס׳ של״ה אבל יקרא בו מ״ש בתוכחת מוסר... מ״ש בדרשות... וכן חובה כאשר עשיתי זה אשתקד ובלי נדר עוד דעתי לעשות בזה״ז ללמוד עם תלמידים בחורים וב״ב טרם פתחי ללמד עמם שיעור בגמ׳ או סופק ללמד עמם דף אחד משל״ה למען ידעו כי לא המדרש עיקר אלא המעשה... ("יערות דבש", ה"א, דרשה י״ב).

99. *Mezaref Avodah*, p. 23 – דכשאדם עוסק בתורה כל היום א״צ ללמוד ספרי מוסר כלל כאשר שמעתי מרבינו שפ״א בקשו ממנו שיגיד דברי מוסר והשיב בדרך שחוק אין מכים לתינוק אלא בשביל שילך לבית הספר אבל אחר שילך ה א״צ להכותו כן כל ספרי מוסר מוכיחים על לימוד התורה והלומד כל היום א״צ למוסר כלל.

The author appends the parenthetical note: אמר המס׳ כן שמעתי מפי ר׳ סעדי׳ תלמידו. The מסדר or compiler is in all probability identical with the author of this apocryphal work. R. Saadiah, one of the key anti-Hasidic controversialists, was a student of the Gaon and immigrated to the Holy Land with other students of the Gaon in 1809–1810. He was a brother-in-law of R. Shelomoh Zalman, the brother of R. Ḥayyim (D.Z. Hilmann, "אגרות בעל-התניא" [Jerusalem, חמו"ל, 1953], p. 98, end n. 6). The entire incident, if it ever did occur, sounds much more like R. Ḥayyim, who was concerned with the problem, than like the Gaon, whose writings evince no special interest in it. One may conjecture that the incident described occurred to R. Ḥayyim and that the author, who may have heard it from R. Saadiah, ascribed it to the Gaon as a literary polemical device in the context of the rest of the book.

100. In a conversation with R. Joseph Zondel Salanter, cited by R. Isaac Blazer in his "אור ישראל," p. 24. See D. Katz, "תנועת המוסר," vol. I, p. 91.

101. *Avot* 2:9.

102. *Ruaḥ Ḥayyim* (on 2:9), p. 35. See nn. 94, 97 above.

103. R. Israel Salanter is normally considered the founder of the movement, in the sense that he introduced what was for R. Joseph Zondel a personal mode of pious conduct into the public domain and began to seek adherents; thus Katz, "תנועת המוסר," II, p. 137. H.L. Gordon ("הדואר,"

December 11, 1964, p. 88) considers R. Joseph Zondel the originator of *Musar* in that he advocated its study as a regular part of the curriculum, and R. Isaac Blazer as the most powerful figure in the dissemination of its doctrines and influence.

104. Katz, "תנועת המוסר" vol. I, pp. 86–91.

105. *Ibid.* p. 87. But see n. 114 below.

106. *NH* 4:7; n. 43 above.

107. *NH* 4:9 כי לא הורשה לעסוק בהתבוננות וקניית היראה אלא כפי אשר ישקול בשכלו. Unquoted לפי טבעו לענינו, שזה העת הוא צורך והכרחי לו, לעסוק בקניית היראה והמוסר by Blazer is the rest of the passage: לצורך השימור והקיום של תבואת התורה.

108. R.I. Blazer, "אור ישראל," p. 24. In effect, this prepares the way for *Musar* to replace Halakhah as the principal subject of the curriculum and the goal of the study of Torah. H.L. Gordon, writing from his personal experience as a student in the Musarite Yeshivah כנסת בית ישראל in Slobodka, maintains that when *Musar* was introduced into the academies it tended to overwhelm all else and displace talmudic studies as the central subject ("הדואר," December 18, 1964, pp. 108 f).

109. *Ibid.*

110. *NH* 4:1; see n. 88 above.

111. *Ibid.*: הנה כן דרכו של היצר מעולם להתקנא בעם ה' אלה, כאשר המה דורכים בדרך ה' כראוי, להטיל בהם ארס, עד שכמה מהתלמידים שמו כל קביעותם ועסקם רק בפלפולה של תורה לבד ולא זולת כלל, ושנינו במשנתינו אם אין יראה אין חכמה.

112. Katz, "תנועת המוסר" vol. I, p. 88. Katz has been severely criticized, especially for his history of the movement prior to World War I, by H.L. Gordon, who cites a number of personal experiences to underscore Katz's unreliability in the early history of *Musar* ("הדואר," December 11, 1964, pp. 88–90; December 18, 1964, p. 108 f).

113. *Ibid.*, p. 89.

114. Ch. Zaichyk, "המאורות הגדולים", 2nd ed. (New York: Balshan, 1962), p. 119. Also quoted, in approximately the same manner, in "חיי המוסר," (Bene-Berak, 1964), vol. II, no. 209, p. 37. The reversal of roles attributed to the evil urge brings the Musarites, in this respect, quite close to the Hasidim as opposed to R. Ḥayyim: cf. n. 94 above.

115. Gedaliahu Alon, "מחקרים בתולדות ישראל" (1957), p. 6; Rabbi J.B. Soloveitchik, *loc. cit.*, p. 698.

116. While R. Ḥayyim remains consistent throughout in theory, his concessions in practice – and they are frequent – introduced considerable ambiguity into his position; thus, e.g., his allowance for brief devotional periods in the midst of one's study (n. 43 above), which left him open to misinterpretation, or at least reinterpretation, by R. Isaac Blazer (n. 108

above); his allowance for laymen (n. 97 above), and so on. It is probably this attempt at reconciling the conflicting and legitimate demands of both scholarship and piety that left the erroneous impression that R. Ḥayyim had not developed a firm and consistent point of view, and that allowed opposing schools to read their own ideas into his words. The implications of this unintended vagueness were to be spelled out much later when the famous student "strike" occurred at Volozhin. The strike, which lasted for three months, was directed against the spiritual overseer (משגיח) R.A. Droshkovitz, during the incumbency of R. Raphael Shapiro as the head of the school, i.e., after the Yeshivah of Volozhin had been "officially" closed by the government (see R.H.R. Rabinowitz, "הדואר", vol. XLII, no. 18 [March 2, 1962], 275, and as corrected in later issues by J. Matlov, vol. XLII, no. 20 [March 16, 1962], 317, and I. Rivkind, vol. XLII, no. 23 [April 6, 1962], 367). Matlov (*loc. cit.*) adds that a maxim of the striking students was אין מולחין מלח במלח, i.e., it was unnecessary to strengthen the influence of Torah in the Yeshivah by external means, *Musar* study, since the students already were studying Torah. This position unquestionably accords with R. Ḥayyim's basic teachings. The most prominent rabbis of the day were against the introduction of *Musar* into the curriculum possibly because they harbored a powerful fear and suspicion of sectarianism; nevertheless, *Musar* soon infiltrated the great Lithuanian academies and, in fact, served as a timely antidote to the growing Haskalah movement (A. Kariv, *loc. cit.*, p. 12; G. Alon, *op. cit.*, pp. 5 f.) The very success of the movement was its undoing. *Musar* study became so popular in the schools that accepted it that the study of Halakhah suffered. It was on this account that R. Isaac Blazer, who more than anyone else was responsible for this imbalance, was condemned by a rabbinical convocation in 1897 (H.L. Gordon, "הדואר", December 11, 1964, p. 90). These perils were clearly foreseen by R. Ḥayyim, as were parallel similar developments in Hasidism.

Knowing vs. Learning: Which Takes Precedence?*

EDUCATION IS THE LIFEBLOOD OF JUDAISM. "THE STUDY of Torah outweighs them all" (*Pe'ah* 1:1). There are several *mitzvot* that the Sages said "outweigh them all," but clearly Torah study has the greatest place of eminence in the hierarchy of Jewish values.[1] R. Ḥayyim of Volozhin taught in his *Nefesh ha-Ḥayyim* that it is not that Torah study is on one side, while all the other *mitzvot* are on the other side, and Torah study is weightier than the others. Rather, Torah study is the entity from which all others radiate. They are the part, of which Torah study is the whole.[2] This gives Torah study a completely different status. It is not something apart from *mitzvot*. It is the origin of all *mitzvot*.

The Sages asked, "Which is greater, *talmud* (study) or *ma'aseh* (action)?" They concluded, "Study is greater, since it leads to action" (*Kiddushin* 40b). One who does not know Torah cannot practice the *mitzvot* properly. That is why they said, "An ignoramus cannot be pious" (*Avot* 2:6). An ignoramus cannot know that which he needs to practice as a Jew. Torah

---

* This essay by Rabbi Lamm appeared in *Wisdom From All My Teachers: Challenges and Initiatives in Contemporary Torah Education*, edited by Jeffery Saks and Susan Handelman (Jerusalem: Urim Publications, 2003), pp. 15–23. It is reprinted here with permission of ATID (Academy for Torah Initiatives and Directions).

knowledge has a clear place in the general structure of the values of Torah.

The question is: which is more important, Torah study or Torah knowledge? Clearly, Torah study (*Limmud*) is exceedingly important, and so is Torah knowledge (*yedi'ah*). But is there more importance to learning as a process, or to knowing as a passive achievement?

If Torah knowledge is the totality and ultimate aim of Torah, then it might be possible sometime in the future to fulfill one's obligation of Torah study by purchasing a microchip that contains all 400 books of responsa from the Bar Ilan CD-ROM and implanting it in one's brain. One would have Torah knowledge. What more would one need? There are other shortcuts that technology might invent, by which one could achieve a great deal of knowledge without spending terribly much energy in acquiring that knowledge. So the question is: which will it be?[3]

Judaism vs. The Greeks

This question has certain clear philosophic underpinnings. It goes back to the days when Judaism was involved in a struggle with Hellenism and the teachings of Greek civilization. The Jewish struggle with the Greeks was not only a physical battle. We won that battle, so we celebrate Hanukkah.[4] But it was also a conflict in the world of ideas and values, and that has many consequences.

Scholars tell us that Plato, whose writings are the origin of so much of Western philosophical thought throughout the ages, posed an ontological question, that is, a question about the very nature of reality. He said that there was a difference between *being* and *becoming*. Becoming means development, constant growth, progress. Being means the aim, the end result. Greek thought, starting with Plato, said that being trumps becoming.[5] Being is the ideal, and becoming is just the means toward achieving that ideal. The end is the more important. The word "end" in English, like the word *"takhlit"* in Hebrew, has two meanings – it means the final item or part, and also means the purpose, as in "means and ends." Since the purpose is greater than what leads to it, being takes precedence over becoming. Accordingly, the Greeks believed that knowledge is the ultimate goal because it is a state of being.

In his *Shemonah Perakim*,[6] Maimonides poses a similar question. Who is greater, he asks: the righteous person who was born with perfect character (*he-hasid ha-me'uleh*), or the one who struggles with his own evil inclination and overcomes it (*ha-kovesh et yitzro*)? Maimonides answers that the Greek philosophers taught us that the one who was born perfect is preferable, because a person who already has his perfection is the ideal for which we aim. This fits in beautifully with the Greek concept that being is superior to becoming. But, he continues, the Jewish sages prefer the one who is constantly involved in the struggle with his own self, with his own darker forces, and overcomes them. That is much more virtuous than the one who was effortlessly well behaved all along. Interestingly, Maimonides himself tries to reconcile the differences. In some ways he prefers the one who was born perfect; in others, the one who overcomes himself. But he concedes that the Jewish sages hold that the one who overcomes himself is greater than the one who was born perfect; the struggle is more precious than the prize.

We may, I believe, find precedent for this clash of ideas in the biblical narrative concerning the conflict between Yosef and Yehudah. Yosef is well behaved all along, a favorite or darling of his father. He is unselfconsciously a leader, and does the right thing almost all the time. (Even when we find a struggle, in Yosef's encounter with Potiphar's wife, it is one in which he ultimately does the right thing.) He seems to be much closer to the prototype who was born perfect. But Yehudah is different. At the same time that Yosef is sold into slavery, starting a series of events that elevate him to become the viceroy of Egypt, we read, "At that time Yehudah descended" (Gen. 38:1). Yehudah becomes involved with a woman whom he takes to be a harlot, and she turns out to be his daughter-in-law. Also, he previously said, "What profit is there in killing our brother?" – we might as well sell him (Gen. 37:26–27). Yehudah appears as a man who is beset by less-than-noble impulses. When Tamar shows Yehudah that he is the owner of the tokens he gave her when he thought her a harlot, she asks him, "Recognize this?!" (Gen. 38:25). It is the same expression that the brothers – and probably Yehudah himself – had used when speaking to Ya'akov: "Recognize this? Is this your son's multicolored coat?" (Gen. 37:32). What is Yehudah's reaction? He sees the challenge and overcomes it. He says, "She is right and I am wrong" (Gen. 38:26). Later, he rises to the occasion when he confronts Yosef (whom he does not recognize as Yosef), and, in offering his own life instead of Benjamin's, he shows greatness. This explains why Ya'akov, on his deathbed, speaks lovingly of Yosef but of Yehudah says, "Yehudah is a lion's cub, my son, you ascended from prey (*teref*)" (Gen. 49:9). Rashi asks: what is "*teref*"? It is based on the words, "*Tarof toraf Yosef* – Yosef has surely been torn apart" (Gen. 37:33). Yehudah, who led Ya'akov to believe that Yosef had been torn apart by a wild beast, has risen above all that. Instead of "Yehudah descended," it is "you ascended." There is a great sense of growth in Yehudah. This is an example of the contrast between the one who was born perfect and the one who overcomes himself, with the one who overcomes himself taking precedence.

Judaism, then, adopts a worldview diametrically opposed to that of the Greeks and holds that becoming takes precedence over being. Accordingly, we believe that study is more important than knowledge. If knowledge is a state of being, studying is an act of becoming. As one studies, he keeps growing and growing. There is always movement toward the goal of knowledge. The process, the becoming, is what the studying is all about. In Judaism, the active process, the experience of learning, is valued more than passive knowledge. Torah study is greater than Torah knowledge, because becoming is greater than being. That is why, although a scholar of the Talmud is called a *ḥakham* (wise person), the term we usually use is *talmid ḥakham* (student of the wise). A *ḥakham* is one who knows; a *talmid ḥakham* is one who learns. Similarly, a *lamdan* (a master of Torah study) is not one who knows, but one who learns, in the same way that a *gazlan* (a thief) is not one who knows how *to* steal, but one who actually steals. The passion for learning is more important than knowing.[7]

Practical Implications

This preference for the process explains what the Sages mean when they say (*Avot 5:26*), "According to the pain is the reward." What one is rewarded for is the pain involved in the process – the pain of studying, the pain of researching, the pain of thinking, the pain of solving conflicts, the pain of being confronted by one's own ignorance and struggling to overcome it. King Solomon says, "The one who adds knowledge adds pain" (Eccles. 1:18). Rabbi Menahem Mendel of Kotzk, one of my favorite sources of hasidic wisdom and wit (not in the humorous sense, but in the sense of intelligence), comments, "*krenken zolst du, aber lernen musst du* – "Though you shall become sick, still you must learn!"[8] Torah is acquired through suffering; there is no easy way out. If a person wants to achieve anything in the life of Torah, he needs to invest his peace of mind, health, concentration and focus.[9] Five hundred years ago, one of the giants of Ashkenazic Jewry, R. Yisrael Isserlein (the author of *Terumat ha-Deshen*), wrote about some of his students who came from wealthy homes. They had a new invention that they brought into the *beit midrash*: a type of turntable. Instead of standing up and walking over to the shelf to get a book, they would place all their *Gemarot* and other volumes on the "lazy Susan." They were able to learn with greater ease. They had a shortcut. R. Isserlein comments as follows, "Those rich, pampered students ... are not acting properly. On the contrary! When someone seeks a book and gets it with great effort, because of that [effort] he will remember what he wants to learn."[10] If one invests pain and effort in learning something in the book, he will remember what he learned. If it comes easy, then easy come, easy go.[11]

To my mind, the most amazing example of the traditional emphasis on study as opposed to knowledge comes to us from a rather arcane book. One of the most difficult, the most recondite, abstract, and abstruse parts of the Zoharic literature is the small volume, *Sifra deTzeni'uta*. The Gaon of Vilna wrote a commentary, equally difficult, on the *Sifra de-Tzeni'uta*. It was published with an introduction by the Gaon's student, R. Hayyim of Volozhin. There R. Hayyim records astounding biographical items about the Vilna Gaon. It is well known that the Gaon was already a great genius in his youth. But he also lived an exceedingly rich mystical life. Now R. Hayyim was no fantasy-spinning Hasidic rebbe; he was a sober Litvak, very careful, measured, and precise about what he said. Yet the Gaon told R. Hayyim that, from the time he was nine years old, he had had *aliyyot neshamah* (spiritual experiences) every night, which continued for about seventy years. He received mystical visitations from Ya'akov Avinu, from Moshe Rabbeinu, and of course from Eliyahu ha-Navi. One day the Gaon called R. Hayyim in and said, "Go see Zelmele.[12] Tell him that tonight he will have an angelic visitation of *maggidim*.[13] They will offer him solutions to all the problems that he is having in his Torah study. Tell him to chase them away, because any Torah knowledge which comes without the toil of Torah study is not worth it." The Gaon did not say they would offer false information. They would offer correct information, but it should not be accepted. Any Torah knowledge that is easily acquired is simply not Torah; it has no spiritual or moral value. The value of one's Torah knowledge is directly proportionate to the energy, the suffering, and the hard experience of acquiring it. The more one has invested in becoming, the more will he achieve in the realm of being.

The dispute we have seen between Judaism and Hellenism has certain surprising results. When the Greeks spoke about education, they usually had in mind adults, not children. The only reason a child needed to learn was as preparation for being an adult. An indication of the Greeks' priorities appears in a Greek word which midrashic literature borrows: *"pedagogue."* The pedagogue was a teacher, but was usually a slave as well – a knowledgeable slave whom the master would use to teach his children. In Judaism, the relationship goes the other way around: the teacher is called a *rav*, a master. There is a very interesting counterpoint here. For the Greeks, the children's teacher was usually only a slave. In Judaism, the children's teacher is an important master. Interestingly, in Maimonides' *Hilkhot Talmud Torah*, the first three *halakhot* deal almost exclusively with the education of children. (For example: the father must teach the child; if the father is absent, who teaches the child?) Only in the fourth *halakhah* does Maimonides finally state that just as it is a *mitzvah* to teach children, so too it is a *mitzvah* to teach oneself. Learning by oneself as an adult is in a sense derivative of the requirement to teach one's children. For Judaism, teaching children becomes more important than teaching adults. Why? Although the end product is considered important, the process – the study – is much more important. Teaching demands more insistent and persistent effort than educating oneself. This explains why, generally, our priority is child education, as opposed to adult education.

To summarize, we have an encounter of two different worldviews, and the consequences thereof. The Greek worldview valued being over becoming, so it emphasized the end product, the knowledge acquired by adults. The Jewish worldview gives full value to Torah knowledge, without which one cannot perform *mitzvot*, but it ascribes greater value to Torah study, the process of acquiring that knowledge. Accordingly, Judaism emphasizes child education and the greatness of a teacher as a master, one who is responsible for educating the next generation.

The Struggle of Teaching

As I am somewhat involved in the field of education, I know that teachers are very often frustrated. There is a very high degree of burnout. It is not easy to be a teacher. Therefore, educators frequently fret. I have heard this from many teachers in elementary schools, in high schools, and even in universities. They complain that they put so much effort into teaching and yet they do not produce the desired results. They do not see the students getting as much as they should out of school. They feel frustrated by not being able to fulfill their educational goals. Both the quantity learned and the joys of learning are less than they ought to be. The struggle is often a very disheartening one.

Nevertheless, we who dedicate our careers and lives to educating the next generation need to remember this principle: the process is more important than the results. The very act of teaching, the struggle of challenging the students, is worthwhile even if it does not succeed in the way the teacher would like, and even if it appears to fall on deaf ears. Who is to say that as circumstances change and children's minds mature and expand, today's ignored lessons will not be recalled with nostalgia and verve? Our work remains sacred even when our labors seem in vain. Success should be measured not by our students' gain in knowledge but by their desire to learn more. That is the point of our craft, of our profession, of our call, of our commitment.

Two statements can illustrate the importance of the struggle. The first is by R. Shneur Zalman of Lyady, known as the *Ba'al ha-Tanya*. He addresses the struggle we all have, the eternal war between the evil inclination and the good inclination. It can be discouraging, because the evil inclination too often is the victor.[14] The *Ba'al ha-Tanya* writes, "A person must not let his heart sink or be depressed, even if this war continues for his whole lifetime. Perhaps it is for this that he was created, and this is his service [of God]."[15] The same holds true for any kind of worthy struggle in which we are engaged – whether it is the struggle between our base passions and our yearning for the good and the true and the sacred, or the struggle involved in teaching, or the struggle of maintaining one's balance in Judaism while confronting the secular world (a struggle in which all of us are engaged). It may be frustrating and it may be painful. Nevertheless, the *Ba'al ha-Tanya* advises, we must not lose heart, we must not complain, because it is not the achievement and the end, but the means, the very act of struggle to which the greatest virtue adheres.

The Talmud states, "If someone tells you, 'I struggled but I did not reach my goal,' do not believe it" (*Megillah* 6b). R. Menahem Mendel of Kotzk comments, "The struggle itself is already an achievement of the goal." Even if one has not achieved what he wanted, as long as he struggles he has won. The final product is secondary. We must not believe the one who says "I did not reach my goal," because he does not realize that the goal is secondary. Rather, "I struggled and succeeded – believe him." We must believe that the attempt to achieve is what the Torah and the moral life are all about.

This is the relationship of knowing and learning. Without denying the crucial value of knowing, learning has primacy. It is the struggle that is the source of our heroism, our value, and our contribution.

Notes

1. Not only R. Hayyim of Volozhin, who was the leading student of the Vilna Gaon, and therefore the ideological spokesman for the mitnagdic point of view, but even *hasidut* and *hasidim* agree with this. This is very much counter to the popular prejudice, that *hasidim* were all lower-class people or commoners, who were not sufficiently intellectually inclined to be *talmidei hakhamim*. That is a rather crass prejudice, as there were many distinguished Torah scholars from the hasidic world. A story about R. Avraham Bornstein (the Sochatchover Rebbe, author of the *Avnei Nezer*) is indicative of the value placed by *hasidim* on Torah study. When he was older, he became ill. The doctors commanded him to stay in bed, and added that he must not study Torah, because when he did study he would get so involved that he would exert himself, and it was liable to bring premature death. When they told him this, he replied that he was going to study anyway. They said, "Rebbe, it is a matter of life or death." He retorted, "If I learn Torah, then I will die. But if I do not learn Torah, I am going to die. I would rather die from learning Torah than from not learning Torah."

2. R. Hayyim of Volozhin, *Nefesh ha-Hayyim* 4:29.

3. In the following analysis, I elaborate on the approach I previously developed in "Education in Israel and in the United States," *Ten Da'at* 8:1 (Spring 1995): 11–14.

4. Actually, we may have lost part of the battle, because the question then was assimilation, and unfortunately assimilation is still very much a part of Jewish society.

5. This appears, among other places, in the allegory of the cave. See Plato, *The Republic*, book VII: 518–19.

6. *Shemonah Perakim*, chap. 6.

7. A personal anecdote may illustrate the point. I recall, as a young man, coming with high anxiety to the class of the late Rabbi Soloveitchik. He was extremely demanding. We would come into his class ready for intellectual battle – and we shriveled up. We would put our *Gemarot* in front of our faces and peek over them, so he would not recognize us and call on us. Unfortunately, he very often caught me. I remember once, when he had been developing a thesis for some time, he asked me, "Lamm, what does *Tosfos* say?" I was intimidated, so I repeated what he had said the previous day. I thought, "He is going to be pleasantly surprised." But he erupted like a volcano, and said to me, "I know what *I* am saying. I do not need you to tell me! What do *you* think?" His greatness as a teacher was that he wanted a student to learn to think

along the lines of his method, but not simply repeat his conclusions parrot-like. He valued a student who challenged him over a student who passively received the information. As a matter of fact, he got so angry with me that he added, "They can sell you the Brooklyn Bridge! The problem is that you check your evil inclination outside the classroom door and come in with the good inclination. Next time, bring your evil inclination with you, and leave your good inclination outside!" He wanted a student to use his "evil inclination," his passion, in order to conquer a *Tosafot* and understand it properly. He valued the passion and process of study over knowledge, important as knowledge is. The "correct answer" is secondary to the effort to attain it. That was an experience that I have taken with me throughout my life.

8. Cf. *Emet Mi-Kotzk Titzmaḥ*, ed. Moshe Shenfeld (Benei Berak: Netzah, 1961), #584, commenting on Eccles. 1:18.

9. See *Berakhot* 5a. Taking it one step further, the Ḥazon Ish writes in a letter, "It is my nature to view everything as difficult, and I hardly ever found anything easy." Everything in life is difficult. Nothing is easy. See R. Avraham Yishayahu Karelitz, *Kovetz Iggerot*, ed. S. Greineman (Benei Berak, 1955), vol. 2, #34 (pp. 44–45).

10. R. Yosef ben Moshe, *Leket Yosher*, vol. 2, p. 39, citing R. Israel Isserlein.

11. Another personal anecdote for which I beg the reader's indulgence: When I was a youngster, I needed to save pennies in order to buy a book. I find that what I learned from books I bought then remains with me much longer than what I learn from books I purchase by walking into a bookstore, and easily writing out a check. The investment plays a major role. When I was about sixteen or seventeen, I was learning with my grandfather, R. Yehoshua Baumol, who was a great *posek* (halakhic expert). Somewhere in the beginning of *Pesaḥim*, *Tosafot* quotes a Rashi in *Yevamot*. I read it – "Rashi explains" – and went on. My grandfather interrupted, "Wait a minute. What are you doing?" I said, "I'm reading the *Tosafot*." He asked, "But what is *Tosafot* saying?" I replied, "He's quoting a Rashi in *Yevamot*." He challenged, "Well, how do you know he is telling the truth? Maybe *Tosafot* is fooling you. Maybe he didn't read it correctly." My grandfather continued, "I want to tell you something: When it comes to *emunot ve-de'ot* (theology), you have to be a *ma'amin* (believer). When it comes to learning, you have to be an *apikores* (heretic)! One needs to challenge everyone, one needs to be a skeptic. If *Tosafot* claims that Rashi says so, get up – don't be lazy, learn that Rashi, and make sure *Tosafot* is telling the truth." As

everyone knows in the world of scholarship, that is the way to genuine achievement. One needs a skeptical attitude, and that means investing a lot of energy and time.

12. Zelmele was the nickname of R. Shelomo Zalman, the younger brother of R. Hayyim. Zelmele died young, at the age of thirty-three. A contemporary of his maintained that had Zelmele lived to a ripe old age, he might have exceeded the Gaon of Vilna himself. See Y.L. Maimon, *Sarei ha-Me'ah* (Jerusalem: Mosad ha-Rav Kook, 1965), vol. 2, p. 131.

13. *Maggidim* refer, in this context, to a type of paranormal phenomenon in which the mystic has his own voice speak from within him without his conscious control. In the sixteenth century, R. Yosef Karo, the author of the *Shulhan Arukh*, would have a visitation from a *maggid* every Friday night. After eating and saying the Grace after Meals, he would put his head down and go into a type of trance, and the *maggid* would tell him Torah thoughts. R. Karo describes this in his book, *Maggid Meisharim*.

14. R. Yisrael Salanter once said that the evil inclination is compared to a fly. A person chases it away, and it comes right back again.

15. R. Shneur Zalman of Lyady, *Likkutei Amorim (Tanya,* chap. 27).